# The Book of Unusual Sports Knowledge

Bruce Miller and Team Golfwell

Cover by King of Designer. Images are from creative commons except where indicated.

ISBN 9798877321991 Hardback black and white

***"Sports teaches you character, it teaches you to play by the rules, it teaches you to know what it feels like to win and lose. It teaches you about life.***

**-- Billie Jean King**

**Think you've heard it all?** So, you think you've heard every strange but true story from the wide world of sports, do you?

Not so fast, sports fans. The annals of athletic competition are filled with tales of the unexpected, surprising and downright extraordinary tales of sports. And we've dug up some doozies for you along with some that are rare and fascinating.

From baseball players cursed by goats, soccer matches that featured witch doctors, the MMA fighter who knocked himself out and woke up the winner of the match, to surfing gigantic tsunami waves in the Pacific Ocean, the stories we've uncovered will surprise and delight even the most ardent sports fan.

*Charles Barkley threw a bad guy through a plate glass window in a bar in Orlando. Learn why he did it and what he told the judge when being sentenced.*

*A jockey died while in the saddle during a horse race and the horse wound up winning the race by a head length with the deceased jockey still on his back.*

*A referee attacked a player he was supposed to protect during a hockey game.*

You will find the answers on these pages along with intriguing facts your friends won't believe, plus a few sports quizzes, and much more!

So, find a comfy seat, grab some snacks, and get ready for a surprise or two by the fascinating, and unusual sports stories in this book!

**Jockey Dies in the Saddle But Still Wins.** There are many ways one can graduate from this life, but the most fortunate are those that join the departed while doing what they loved.

Horse racing is one of humanity's oldest sport competitions. Called the "the sport of kings", history shows not that many kings themselves dominated in racing horses. Perhaps it got the nickname because royalty loved to watch the intense action?

It's not hard to do. The fastest horse wins over a certain distance. That's how it's been ever since people rode on horses. It is still and will always be an adrenaline rush if you ride or full of thrills just watching those amazing animals run!

The horse is obviously the star of the show in horse racing. But the jockey plays such a vital role in whether a horse can achieve its full potential. Jockeys have to ride in an incredible way that minimizes their horses' energy loss with each stride.

Talk about a tough job! It's so demanding that jockeys have even suffered heart attacks or died from the sheer exertion. One jockey's story is truly unbelievable - he expired mid-race but still won despite becoming one of the departed by the time the horse reached the finish line!

Frank Hayes trained horses and worked in the stables. In 1923, the owner asked Frank to ride his horse in an epic steeplechase at Belmont Park racetrack just east of the Big Apple. His horse, Sweet Kiss, was a huge 20:1 underdog. Between that and it being Hayes' racing debut, nobody expected much from man or beast.

But they were in for a shock - a double shock! To make weight, Hayes had to drop an intense 12 pounds in just one day. He pushed himself to the limit jogging it off. By post time, he was wiped out.

Being a jockey is no joke - their bodies work overtime like pistons as their heart rates skyrocket. During the race, Hayes had a severe heart attack and unfortunately died instantly.

Incredibly, he didn't fall off! He stayed put in the saddle, crossing the finish line in first place! The horse won by a head length! Officials were stunned to discover the winner had sadly left this world.

Hayes became the only dead jockey to ever win a race - what an unbelievable story! As for Sweet Kiss, it never raced again but lived on in racing lore as the steed behind the "Sweet Kiss of Death". [1]

Frank Hayes

**The mixed martial arts fighter who knocked himself out and still won**. Most will never find themselves in a boxing ring or in a mixed-martial arts (MMA) match. That said, even the meekest bookworm who has never been in a fight in their life understands on a basic level that the goal is to not be knocked spark out cold.

The fight involved Irvins "The Hammer" Ayala and Drew "The Flippy" Chatman and it ended in spectacular fashion when the lights went out for one scrapper.

Now while getting laid out in the ring is nothing out of the ordinary in an MMA match, this match had a real doozy of an ending.

What made this Ayala vs Chatman throwdown truly bizarre wasn't just that someone got sparked -- fights end in KOs all the time. No, the really wacky thing was that one of the fighters who ended up unconscious actually knocked himself out! And somehow still walked away the winner!

As if a self-KO victory wasn't strange enough, MMA Fighting reports that the story of this 2018 bout gets even weirder.

This donnybrook between Ayala and Chatman was part of the undercard for 36 fights scheduled that night in California. During one exchange, Chatman found himself on his back when Ayala came charging in with a nasty hammer fist strike and Ayala was well-known for the hammer fist.

But in a bizarre twist of fate, as Ayala was bringing the hammer down, he somehow managed to smash his own chin clean on Chatman's knee, instantly knocking himself out!

While self-KOs aren't unheard of apparently, this was a real head-scratcher.

With Ayala taking a nap, the ref called the fight - but wait, it was about to get even wackier! Because as Chatman began celebrating his apparent victory, that's when things went totally off the rails!

Even though Irvins "The Hammer" Ayala had only been conscious for a few minutes in the first round before smashing his own lights out, he was somehow declared the winner!

The reason? When the match was stopped, Drew "The Flippy" Chatman decided to showboat by attempting a backflip off Ayala's prone body. Bad move!

The ref took major exception to Chatman's unsportsmanlike grandstanding and reversed the decision, awarding the wacky win to the still-unconscious Ayala!

He should have taken the advice of Bruce Lee who said, "Showing off is the fool's idea of glory."

"The Flippy" later issued an apology, saying that was not a good move on his part. No kidding, Mr. Flip. There is a short video of this on the YouTube referenced in the endnotes. [2]

**Fishing.** Joe had the worst luck ever trying to catch just one fish. But nothing after a whole day. On his way home, sweaty and disappointed, he rolled up to the market thinking he had to bring home something.

So, he stops at the fish market and asks for the 4 largest snapper and tells the man behind the counter, “Throw them at me.”

The fish counter guy says, “Why?”

"So, I can honestly tell the wife I actually caught something today.”

The guy says, “Okay, but I suggest that you take the salmon.”

“Why's that?”

“Because your wife stopped in earlier today and said that if you came by, I should tell you to take salmon. That's what she'd like for supper tonight,” replied the guy with a smile.

**“It’s just a job,”** Muhammad Ali had a genius for expressing himself clearly. One of his famous quotes was, “Grass grows, birds fly, waves pound the sands. I beat people up.” He certainly did his job well!

**Gym mishap**. At the gym, a guy was in the medicine ball area. Inadvertently, he picked up a bounce ball instead of the leather medicine ball (he must have had a lot on his mind since he didn't immediately notice the difference). Anyway, he picked it up and raised it above his head and gave it a mighty slam into the floor and, of course, the ball bounced up and smacked him right in the face. I had to hold back by laughter.

Lesson learned -- study the areas before you start throwing your weight around! He received automatic mind clarity from whatever was bothering him after that ball bounced in the face!

**How is the Super Bowl Stadium Chosen Every Year?** It used to be the warmer cities, and the warmer climates of Miami, New Orleans, and Los Angeles have seen them lead the way with the number of Super Bowls held there. For example, the Greater Miami area, New Orleans, and the LA area have hosted on many occasions.

While weather was previously a primary factor, it is no longer the sole determining criterion. Instead, bidding cities must now engage in a competitive process to earn the responsibility and honor of hosting the big game.

This bidding procedure has changed. In the past, the National Football League (NFL) would directly invite select cities to submit formal proposals. From the submitted bids, the league would narrow the options down to a few "finalists" who would then be asked to present their proposals in-person.

These comprehensive presentations - often exceeding 600 pages in length and requiring around a year to compile - would then be thoroughly reviewed by the 32 team owners, who would ultimately decide upon the winning venue. In recent years this has changed.

Beginning in 2018, the NFL opted to forgo the large-scale bidding competition. Instead, the league proactively contacts pre-selected venues and requests they develop suitable hosting proposals.

After going through the proposals, it is up to the owners to approve or not approve each one. The host city and venue must fulfill various requirements to be deemed eligible. The host stadium should be located in a market with an NFL franchise and have a certain minimum seating capacity of say 70,000 seats. It should have the necessary media and electrical infrastructure to produce a high-caliber Super Bowl broadcast. Stadiums in cities with average game-day temperatures which aren't warm, say below 50 degrees F, are best if they have a roof.

Of course, there has to be ample parking for thousands of vehicles near the stadium. Additionally, the host stadium is expected to have adequate space for the whole gameday

Superbowl experience, including space for an area where there is entertainment within walking distance of the stadium.

The media is extremely important and close attention is made to make sure there is ample space nearby for the Media Center as well as other Super Bowl week events, including golf courses and other activities.

The host city and venue are further responsible for ensuring the necessary infrastructure is in place around all Super Bowl facilities, including parking, security, electrical systems, media infrastructure, communications networks, and transportation solutions. A minimum number of hotel rooms - equal to a certain percentage (say 35%) of the stadium's capacity - must be available within an hour's drive.

Comparable practice facilities, including at least one grass field and one field with the host stadium's surface, should be accessible within a 20-minute drive of team hotels.

Spaces for rehearsals for entertainment events are to be located nearby te stadium as well. Future Super Bowl venues that have already been designated include Allegiant Stadium in Paradise, Nevada for Super Bowl LVIII.

It's a lengthy process that changes from time to time, but decisions are made years in advance to give fans a chance to buy tickets for this amazing event each year.

**Confidence**. The great Larry Bird looked at his opponents in the locker room before the NBA three-point contest and asked them, "Who's coming in second?"

Larry Bird

## The Climber Who Scaled Everest in Shorts.

Wim Hof, also known as the Iceman, lives up to his name. In 1999 he swam under a frozen lake on live TV in Holland.

But that's not all, when someone fell through the ice while watching, he jumped right back in to save them! Can you believe that? Jumping into freezing cold water to rescue someone.

He was just getting started. A few years later in 2007 he climbed almost to the top of Everest wearing just shorts and sandals on his feet. No jacket or anything and set a world record for the highest altitude reached dressed like that.

In total he's broken 26 world records with his crazy stunts. He even ran a marathon in the desert without drinking any water. Insane right?

But doing all this extreme cold weather stuff isn't without risks. He's come close to dying a few times too. Like the time he swam 50 meters under ice in the Arctic and his eyes actually froze over. They had to rescue him after that. He's 57 years old and still at it.

Few wear shorts on cold days. Did you know when David Letterman was asked a question by a reporter wearing shorts on a chilly day if he'd ever do a podcast, Dave replied, "I'd do a podcast about guys wearing shorts when it's too cold."

What was Wim's secret, you might ask? He uses what is now known as the "Wim Hoff Method". It involves some breathing exercises, cold exposure, and mental focus.

The breathing part is called controlled hyperventilation. You do it in sets of 30 to 40 deep breaths. For each breath, you breathe in strongly and breathe out relaxed. On the last breath of each set, you exhale and hold your breath for approximately 1 to 3 minutes or so. Then you take a recovery breath and hold that for 15 seconds.

When you do the rhythmic breathing, it's common to start feeling tingly and weird. Some people even see spots or lights, or get dizzy. I can imagine! It's kind of like meditation breathing in that way. That's probably why Wim says to do it sitting down or lying down, so you don't get too tipsy or dizzy on your feet.

He pushes himself to the limit with his mind over matter approach. You've got to respect someone who can achieve so much through sheer willpower.

Wim Hoff

**Ever notice?** Give a man a fish and you feed him for a day. Give a man another fish and he will be, like, "fish, again?"

Give a man a fish and he will eat for a day. Teach him how to fish, and he will sit in a boat and drink beer all day. Seriously, sitting quietly in total silence fishing with a fishing buddy makes you feel it is one of the best conversations you've ever had.

**Soccer Player Headbutts Own Teammate**. The Colombian soccer scene was rocked by an all-out brawl between supposed teammates. This wasn't the one team brawling with the other team brawl. This was an intra team brawl.

During a crucial late-game free kick for Atletico Nacional, star strikers Dayro "El Toro" Moreno and Jeison "Cabeza Dura" Lucumi got into a heated dispute over who would take the shot.

Eyewitnesses report that Moreno was casually bouncing the ball like a basketball as he strolled up to put the team on his back, when Lucumi came barreling in with his head down like a bull seeing red. Lucumi lowered his dome and charged straight into Moreno's face and gave him a bone crunching.

Referees immediately flashed the red card as Lucumi began headbutting everything in his path, including the corner flag, a ball boy, and the stadium jumbotron.

Moreno, dazed from the brutal headbutt, stumbled around like a drunk until teammates restrained him from going after Lucumi with a flying knee.

After order was restored, Nacional was forced to finish the match with only 10 men. The loss of scoring opportunities from the ejection was surely a factor in the 0-0 final score. Atletico's manager could only shake his head in disbelief at the locker room antics and reportedly said, "These guys need to get their heads checked, literally and figuratively."

It's clear there are still differences between Lucumi and Moreno. Fans can only hope they settle their differences in a sanctioned boxing match rather than further sullying the beautiful game with more head trauma on the pitch.

**Roman Emperor Nero gets into the act**. Nero wasn't known for the Olympics normally, but the notorious Roman emperor was hands down the most successful competitor ever.

Nero reportedly hauled in an unreal 1,800 wreaths - the ancient equivalent of medals - in a single Olympics! In fact, Nero even won a chariot race where his chariot crashed and flipped during the event.

How'd he pull that off? The judges ruled he totally would win, so they declared him the champion anyway.

As it turns out, Nero had always dreamed of becoming an Olympics legend. So, he arranged to delay the games a couple years until his visit to Greece.

He finally made it to Greece in 67AD. Olympics officials were terrified of the mentally unstable man-child who could order their public execution with a snap.

So, judges showered Nero with awards and wreaths for every event he entered, even ones he skipped! They gave him wreaths for singing and lyre playing - which weren't even Olympics categories. But the judges handed them over just to stay on Nero's good side.

**What diversion is exceptionally popular at Wimbledon Tennis?** Almost 200,000 portions of strawberries and cream are served during just two weeks of the tournament. That treat is almost more important than the players, and everything else!

**The Craziest Psychedelic No-hitter Ever Thrown (according to Dock Ellis, anyway).** On June 12, 1970, Pittsburgh Pirates pitcher Dock "the Doctor" Ellis did something truly bonkers -- he tossed a no-hitter against the San Diego Padres while on LSD!

Dock dropped some liquid sunshine earlier in the day and then took the mound in a state of psychedelic bliss.

Now I ask you, how the heck does a man function, let alone dominate on the baseball field, when he's seeing sounds and hearing colors?

But according to Dock, that's what happened! He said he was seeing all sorts of wild stuff like thinking Richard Nixon was behind the plate calling balls and strikes (can you imagine?!). At one point, he thought he was pitching to guitar god Jimi Hendrix instead of an actual baseball player. No wonder he walked eight guys!

After the game, Dock was still flying high as a kite. He remembers diving out of the way of a line drive that wasn't even hit hard! Talk about being lost in the sauce. It's a miracle he didn't try climbing up the outfield wall or something.

Now whether Dock was really tripping balls out there or not is up for debate. He waited over a decade to spill the beans on this acid-fueled achievement. And some folks in the sport have questioned his story. But you gotta admit, if any ballplayer was crazy enough to drop acid and then dominate on the bump, it was the one and only Doctor Dock.

When he wasn't dropping psychedelic bombshells, Dock was blowing minds with his fiery style on the mound. One time he tried to bean every Cincinnati Red just to shake them up. Another time he burned the scouting reports he was supposed to fill out, setting off the sprinklers like a madman. And the Commish had to tell him not to wear curlers on the field!

After hanging up his cleats, Dock got real about helping others with substance issues. Whether his acid no-hitter was real or not, Dock Ellis was one man who always kept you guessing. His legacy lives on as one of baseball's most intriguing and ahead-of-his-time characters.

Dock Ellis

**He had it coming Judge!** Charles Barkley threw a bad guy through a plate glass window in a bar in Orlando, Florida.

You might think this happened in a barroom brawl. No, it was Charles instantly teaching the bad guy a lesson after he threw a glass of ice at the table of the basketball star was sitting at accompanied with three lovely women.

Turned out that the glass of ice hit one of the women sitting with the Charles (the man who threw the glass of ice was later charged with misdemeanor battery).

Charles got up, picked the man up, and threw him through a plate glass window.

Charles was arrested and charged with aggravated battery and resisting arrest without violence.

In his court appearance the judge-imposed community service and a fine on Mr. Barkley. After sentencing, the judge asked him if he had any regrets.

Charles replied that his only regret was that they weren't higher up! We all know violence isn't right, but can you imagine?

**Things thrown at sports matches**. Speaking of throwing things, the Detroit Red Wings are an excellent professional ice hockey team based in the amazing city of Detroit.

For decades, the most die-hard and loyal Detroit Red Wing fans have enthusiastically bought octopuses to excitedly throw onto the ice at several places they play. Those places can be the legendary Joe Louis Arena, historic Olympia Stadium, or the state-of-the-art Little Caesars Arena.

But an octopus? Where did this unusual octopus custom originate from?

According to legendary folklore, the octopus' eight fantastic tentacles perfectly reflect the eight absolutely epic playoff victories that were originally required to victoriously win the coveted Stanley Cup, which is as you know the Championship trophy in the extremely competitive National Hockey League.

This tradition astonishingly dates back to 1952, when the one and only Pete Cusimano, a fish shop owner, uniquely commemorated the first sensational Red Wing score by enthusiastically tossing an octopus with tremendous excitement over onto the ice during the epic third match of the championship series versus the Montreal Canadiens.

"The Wings wonderfully won the game as well as the series, and Cusimano is said to have confidently asserted that his bravely sacrificed octopus played an integral role in the triumphant outcome.

For years, Cusimano showed up with an octopus at each and every Wings home playoff game, powerfully firing it forward onto the ice at the first sensational Red Wing score.

Over the decades, this tradition has somewhat dwindled though there is the occasional die-hard fan sneakily smuggling in an octopus. However, one thing's for certain – this is a tradition that is absolutely unique and can't be found anywhere else on the planet! More unusual things follow.

***Cabbages*** in football (soccer). Steve Bruce was furiously angry after he had a cabbage bravely thrown at him ahead of Aston Villa's dramatic and thrilling 3-3 draw with Preston.

The legendary 57-year-old had a night to forget as Villa amazingly blew a two-lead to trail 3-2 and had the fantastic James Chester sent off, although the sensational Yannick Bolasie's last-minute leveler at least rescued them a point.

Bruce endured chants of "We want Brucie out" from the home faithful and, after the game, powerfully hit out at the fan who bizarrely decided to throw a cabbage at him.

***Rubber Rats***. Panthers are big cats, and you'd think Florida Panthers fans would enthusiastically throw something of a feline nature like a ball of yarn or a squeaky toy, but you'd be only a little right.

Before the 1995-96 season home opener, Panther Scott Mellanby absolutely obliterated a rat in the locker room with a perfectly placed and powerful slap shot and then scored two goals with the same stick. Goalie John Vanbiesbrouck, in a moment of poetic inspiration, called Mellanby's feat a "rat trick".

By the time the playoffs rolled around, Panthers fans were hurling toy rubber rats to the ice for each Panthers goal. The ritual was so nasty and so popular (and so time consuming to clean up) that the NHL established a new rule penalizing home teams for delays of game with similar fan disruptions. The Panthers instead came up with an amazing rat mascot, "Victor E. Rat".

***Catfish.*** Catfish are slimy, stinking and nasty buggers but that hasn't stopped Predator hockey fans from hurling them over the glass and onto the rink. During the 2002-03 season, fans started chucking them onto the ice in response to the Red Wings fans' octopus tradition.

***Fish are a popular choice!*** Harvard and Cornell have a rivalry that started when Harvard people got the idea to tie a live chicken to the goal post making fun of Cornell's School of Agriculture.

Fishing is a big industry in Boston, so Cornell supporters decided it was entirely appropriate to throw fish at the Harvard players during introductions.

Going beyond that, University of New Hampshire fans throw a rotten fish to mark the Wild Cat's first goal, while San Jose Sharks fans have managed, on a couple of occasions, to get actual sharks onto the ice—dead, of course.

***The Flying Leg Incident***. Although most all referees want to be fair to both teams, in the heat of competition, fans get the distinct impression the refs are favoring the other team. Unfair, right? Tell me about it! This one fan was so hopping mad that he decided to lend a leg up to his team.

After watching call after call go against his boys, he'd had enough of the ref's biased whistling. So, he kicked off his prosthetic and launched it onto the ice like a missile. Maybe he hoped it would give his team a fighting chance. Or maybe he just needed to vent some steam! Either way, you've gotta hand it to the guy for taking a stand.

***Chairs***. Famous and highly successful college basketball coach Bobby Knight threw a chair across the Indiana Hoosier court being totally outraged and had to vent to let his anger out.

Bobby, who's in his 80s now, is highly well-loved by many but he didn't care much about what others thought and is known widely for his original comments on sports, like "When my time on earth is gone, and my activities here are passed, I want them to bury me upside down, and my critics can kiss my ass!"

You've gotta love Bobby's fiery spirit. The man was never afraid to get physical if the game wasn't going his way. I can just picture the other coach ducking for cover as a folding chair goes sailing by his head!

***Benches.*** On January 30, 2000, Devils coach Robbie Ftorek decided to take matters into his own hands when Devil Jay Pandolfo was slammed into the boards from behind at high speed while trying to prevent an icing penalty. Surprisingly, no penalty was called, and the Red Wings immediately skated down the ice and scored!

The unfortunate sequence so enraged Ftorek that he heaved one of the team's benches onto the ice. Ftorek was ejected and on top of that received a one-game suspension and a large fine. Devil's player Pandolfo received 84 stitches. But you've gotta admire Ftorek's passion - he was just looking out for his boy! The ref's clearly needed a wakeup call, so Ftorek decided to give them an uncomfortable bench warming.

***Underwear On-Ice.*** The Los Angeles Kings let Jeff Cowan go and cut him from the roster in late 2006. Vancouver picked him up and although Cowan was not known for great offensive play, he gained a quick reputation with Vancouver as one of the league's more daunting players.

Cowan was totally crushing it with his new squad! In just his first four games he lit the lamp six times! The crowd was losing their minds, and after goal number five this one fan just couldn't contain her excitement anymore. You guessed it - she whipped off her bra and tossed it out on the ice! Cowan, soon to be known as "Cowan the Bra-barian", and the team had a good laugh about it. They even signed the bra and auctioned it off. No joke, talk about a story people will remember - this guy was on fire!

They donated the auction proceeds to breast cancer research, as well they should. Talk about scoring big! This fan knew just how to cheer on her man. And good on Cowan for making the most of his new nickname.

Jeff Cowan

**The Fastest Cyclist on the Planet.** Do you remember when you first learned how to ride a bike? Most kids can't believe the ease and speed on a bike after they learn to ride a bike -- especially on a smooth newly paved surface.

According to the Guinness World Records, Dutch cyclist Fred Rompelberg went 167.044 mph (268.828 kph) on the Bonneville Salt Flats in 1995.

Amazing as that is, his record which stood for many years was broken in 2018 by an extraordinary American lady, Denise Mueller-Korenek who is the current world record holder for paced bicycle land speed and she is considered "the fastest cyclist on earth".

Denise's record (and the first and only woman to do this) was also set at the Bonneville Salt Flats in Utah, by traveling an average of almost 184 mph on a custom carbon bike behind a vehicle all of which was designed to lessen the air resistance.

You can see the video on how she did this on YouTube reference in the end notes. [3]

## When the Entire USA Boycotted the Olympics.

Do you know those inspiring Olympic stories of athletes overcoming adversity and accomplishing their wildest dreams? Well, this isn't one of those.

In 1980, President Jimmy Carter threw a massive wrench into the Olympic dreams of America's finest athletes. Why? Because the Soviets had invaded Afghanistan, and President Carter wanted to stick it to them. Making a decision that shocked the world, he announced the U.S. would boycott the Moscow Olympics to protest the invasion.

Overnight, years and years of training went down the drain as 160 American athletes learned they wouldn't be going to the Olympics after all.

"I understand how you feel", Carter reportedly told the crestfallen athletes, and "I thought about it a lot as we approached this moment, when I would have to stand here in front of fine young Americans who trained hard…"

Talk about an understatement. These athletes were, of course, devastated. Some never got another shot at Olympic glory. All because of a political stunt that, as it turned out, didn't accomplish much. The Soviets didn't withdraw from Afghanistan, and in fact, stuck around for another nine years. Carter's move was meant to be a show of moral indignation, but it actually deprived athletes of their lifelong dreams just to make a political point. Not cool. The Olympics are meant to transcend politics, to bring the world together in the spirit of fair play and sportsmanship.

In the end, Carter's boycott was seen as an embarrassing miscalculation. Most other allied nations still competed.

More than forty years later, the 1980 boycott serves as a sobering reminder that politics and sports should rarely mix.

**Fish aren't dumb.** Fishing is a highly popular sport. Fish actually are quite clever creatures! Many scientific studies have been done showing fish have memories, social hierarchies, use tools, and more. The more you know about fish, the better fisherman you become. Here are things you might not have known about fish.

Fish will avoid anything that causes them discomfort or pain, showing that they can learn from past experiences. Our scaly friends know what situations to stay away from. At the same time, fish also know what leads to rewards and will actively pursue opportunities that benefit them.

The experts at the SPCA say that fish possess problem-solving skills too. Can you believe that some fish actually use tools? Certain species like clams, oysters, and mussels tightly close their shells when threatened. But some fish figured out that dropping rocks on these shellfish will force them to open up, revealing a tasty meal inside. These fish essentially discovered how to crack open a safe using the perfect tool.

And let's talk about archerfish - they take intelligence to a whole new level. Not only do they learn to catch their food out of thin air, but they also have an amazing aim and can snatch prey with well-placed shots of water. That's right, archerfish hunt by firing water from their mouths with just the right pressure and volume to knock down targets like insects. They must calculate variables like distance, wind speed, and target size on the fly. The precision and problem-solving abilities of archerfish are truly astounding.

Finding fish - especially smart trout - takes smart searching. While some just cast their line randomly hoping for a bite, that's not how the real pros do it.

The biggest, smartest trout know exactly where to hide to conserve their energy while also staying safe from predators. They lurk in hard-to-reach places like along current seams, under logs, and against the riverbanks and learn how to survive.

They sneak into slow shadowy spots close to obstacles like bushes, grass clumps, rocks and fallen trees. And get this - they sip so lightly you barely see a ripple!

When you think about how fish navigate complex social hierarchies and communicate in schools, it's clear they have some pretty impressive learning faculties. Don't let the scales fool you - underneath lies a mind (about the size of a pea) that's constantly soaking up information. Our scaly friends have some seriously smart schools!

**Sports Quiz Question 1**. The Olympic Games date back more than a thousand years to ancient Greece. What year is officially recognized as the beginning of the Modern Olympic Games?

A. 1896.

B. 1886.

C. 1900.

D. 1906.

*A. on p. 197*

**Crazy about fishing**. One mature wife told a young wife, "Men can become annoying as the years go by. If you want peace now and then, there's fishing. Cook a fish and you feed him for a day. Teach him to fish and you get rid of him for the whole weekend."

**The Curse of the Billy Goat: A Sports Curse on the Chicago Cubs Baseball Team**. The Curse of the Billy Goat was a sports curse that was legendary and diabolically placed on the Chicago Cubs Major League Baseball franchise in 1945, by the one and only Billy Goat Tavern owner William Sianis. This curse lasted an incredible 71 years, from 1945 all the way to the Cubs 2016 championship season.

The curse originated during the epic Game 4 of the 1945 World Series at iconic Wrigley Field, Sianis's pet goat, named Murphy, was causing a ruckus and bothering other fans, so the dynamic duo were asked to leave the ballpark. Some say it was allegedly the Cubs owner Philip K. Wrigley who ordered the ejection due to the goat's odor.

Outraged, Sianis allegedly declared with passion, "Them Cubs, they ain't gonna win no more", which was interpreted as meaning the Cubs would never win another National League pennant, at least for the remainder of Sianis's amazing life.

This curse captured the imagination of Chicago and baseball fans everywhere for decades! What an unbelievable story that shows how much fans care about their beloved teams. And there are conflicting reports that William Sianis attempted to lift the curse before he passed away in 1970, but no one knows for sure.

Finally, after 71 long seasons of heartbreak and disappointment, the Cubs were finally going to get their chance on the grandest stage of them all. It was as if the baseball gods had been waiting for the perfect moment, the perfect time to reward the loyal Cubs fans who had stuck by their team through thick and thin.

And what an incredible moment it turned out to be! On the very anniversary date, the infamous "Billy Goat Curse" had been placed upon Wrigley Field, the Cubs defeated the Dodgers in decisive fashion to win the National League pennant. You could just feel the excitement in the air as those final outs were recorded, with 71 years of frustration melting away. Wrigley Field had never heard cheers so loud!

But the story didn't end there. The Cubs still had one more challenge to face - the AL champion Cleveland Indians. What a matchup it promised to be, with two legendary franchises facing off for baseball's ultimate prize. And what a series it was!

The Cubs as you know won and generations of Cubs fans rejoiced, amazed that they had truly lived to see their Cubbies break the curse and become world champions once again. It was the perfect ending to a story. Those loveable Cubs had done it!

What a thrill it must have been for Cubs fans everywhere when the team finally broke the curse in 2016 to win the World Series after so many years of heartbreak. A true underdog story for the ages!

William Sianis

## The Athlete Who won a Gold Medal in Both the Summer and Winter Olympics.

In 1920, Eddie Eagan became the first, and so far, the only athlete to win gold medals in both the Summer and Winter Olympics in different sports.

Swedish figure skater Gillis Grafström won gold medals in the summer and winter Olympics, but it was the same sport - figure skating. At that time figure skating and ice hockey were events in both the summer and winter Olympics.

How'd Eddie pull it off?

By dominating in two completely unrelated sports: boxing and four-man bobsledding. Talk about a Renaissance man!

After knocking out the competition in Antwerp, Eagan decided 12 years later he'd give those icy tracks a go in Lake Placid. The madman only went and won gold there, too.

Eddie Eagan (1897 - 1967)

**Midway Monster.** The late great Dick Butkus was truly one of a kind. As the original Monster of the Midway, no one played with more intimidation than the legendary middle linebacker for the Chicago Bears.

Between plays, Butkus would let out a low, menacing snarl like a guard dog, letting opponents know the danger that awaited them.

His canine-like tendencies didn't stop there - it was said that in piles of players scrambling for the ball, Butkus had been known to bite an opponent or two.

As if that wasn't scary enough, Butkus was also arguably the most feared tackler to ever play the game. He took it as his personal mission to punish any ball carrier who dared to come into his territory, laying them out with crushing hits on every single down.

Opposing players had to watch their words very carefully when talking about Butkus and the Bears. The man used any perceived slight as extra motivation out on the field.

Running back Altie Taylor of the Detroit Lions learned that lesson the hard way. After their first matchup in 1969, Taylor had called Butkus overrated in an interview.

When the teams met again, Butkus was out for blood. At one point, Taylor was so desperate to avoid a confrontation with the enraged linebacker that he dove into the stands rather than risk Butkus' wrath on the field.

It's easy to see why Butkus struck such fear into opponents. He is one of only three linebackers to be named to multiple All-Decade teams, cementing his status as not only one of the greatest, but also one of the most ferocious players in NFL history.

Most say no one played with the kind of terrifying intensity that Dick Butkus brought to the gridiron every Sunday. Sportswriter Dan Jenkins thought that if it were possible to have all college football teams to have a linebacker like Dick Butkus, then all of the running backs would quickly become three feet tall and sing soprano.

Dick Butkus (1942 - 2023)

**Time out for a joke.** Time out for an old blonde joke you might not have heard.

We all know blondes aren't dumb but take a short break and if you like it, tell it to others but do it at your own risk!

Sam was a handsome man, and he strolled into a Joe's Sport's bar around 9:58pm and takes a seat next to a highly attractive blonde at the bar.

Sam gave her a polite smile as he sat down next to her then got fixed on watching the TV since the 10 pm news was starting.

The news began with a story showing a guy on the very edge of the roof of a tall downtown building looking like he was going to jump and end it all!

The blonde turns to Sam, looks at him, and says, "Think he'll jump?"

Sam says, "Wow! I think he will."

The blonde stares at Sam and says, "Well, I bet he won't."

Sam pulls out his wallet and puts $20 on the bar. "You're on!"

The blonde opens her purse and pulls on a $20 dollar bill but just before she puts it on the bar, the guy jumps off the roof and plummets to his demise!

The blonde's jaw drops then hands Sam the $20 and says, "You win, here's your $20 dollars."

Sam smiles and gives her $20 back and says, "I just can't take your money. I saw this before on the 5pm news and I knew he was going to jump."

The blonde replies, "I did too, but I didn't think he'd do it again."

**Coach Takes 1st Base -- literally.** During a Reds game, the ump called Barry Larkin out at first base to end an inning. Manager Lou Piniella was not happy. He threw his hat on the ground in a huff. That made the ump mad, so he ejected Lou out of the game. Now Lou was really steamed!

Lou yanked the first base right out of the dirt and chucked it across the field. But one throw wasn't enough -- he wound up and launched that sucker again. This time it sailed way over in right field.

"Whoops," said Lou later. "I guess a 46-year-old shouldn't act like such a baby.

The local paper had some fun with Lou's temper tantrum. They held a first base throwing contest in the town square. Lots of folks, including the mayor tried to beat Lou's record throw of 35 feet.

Not too long ago, the same sort of chaos happened when Lloyd McClendon disputed a called out at first base. If you're into stealing bases, check out the YouTube referenced in the end note. [4]

Talk about umpires removing people from the game, if you are wondering what MLB manager holds the record for being ejected from games, that's Bobby Cox with 162 expulsions out of games. In other words, which equates to getting thrown out of every game in a single season!

Most of Bobby's ejections resulted from heated discussions over balls and strikes and first base out calls. Bobby's record most likely will not be broken for some time as he has a big lead over John McGraw in second place with a mere 121 expulsions.

Manager Bobby Cox

**A broken wrist changed the fate of Lebron James.** He said he listens to Beethoven's compositions to relax after lifting weights before a game. The classical music calms him down and gets his mind right.

When Lebron was young, he starred in basketball and football, and learned while suffering from a broken wrist, the healing time can derail your whole career path. He got a broken wrist in 2002 during an AAU basketball game. With two months of recovery needed, it made him choose between football and basketball. He decided to focus on hoops, setting him on the road to the NBA.

Here are some other things you might not be aware of in Lebron's life.

- It wasn't easy growing up for LeBron. At 16, his mom Gloria had him but soon lost her own mom. For six years they couch surfed and lived in apartments in Akron's projects with no support system.

- When LeBron was nine, he met coach Bruce Kelker who started a youth football team. They eventually moved in with Kelker and another coach Frank Walker. After missing so much school due to the instability, LeBron didn't miss a single day in fifth grade.

- To be the best, prioritize rest. LeBron still to this day gets a solid eight hours of sleep every night and takes naps during the day. This is key due to the physical demands of basketball.

- LeBron drinks a small bit of red wine daily for health benefits. Teammate Kevin Love called him a "supercomputer" when it comes to wine knowledge.

- LeBron was the first NBA player on the cover of Vogue magazine in 2008.

- LeBron is actually left-handed but trained himself to shoot with his right. Though not fully ambidextrous, his dedication to developing his non-dominant hand has served him well in his legendary career.

- LeBron's son Bronny is a highly talented basketball player and he’s 17 years old and 6'4". LeBron's hopes he will play with Bronny in the NBA one day. But due to league rules, Bronny is eligible to enter the draft as of 2024. We’ll see what happens!

Lebron James

**The Goalie Who Got Traded for a Bus**. You think you had a weird week at the office? Try being Peter Martin.

There you are, minding your own business playing goalie for the Victoria Cougars junior hockey team, when suddenly you find yourself traded. For a bus.

That's right, in one of the most bizarre deals in hockey history, the Cougars sent you packing to the Seattle Breakers in exchange for an old team bus and $35k in cold hard cash.

Just like that, your childhood dreams of hometown glory on the ice are out the window, and you've got a new nickname to boot: "Bussey." All thanks to some creative wheeling and dealing by management.

So, the next time you're feeling down thinking times are bad remember poor Pete and that things can always get worse. His bosses literally traded him for a used vehicle.

**The Surfer Who Rode Tsunami Waves**. Chris Nel is a New Zealand surfer, who was surfing off the coast of Samoa when the tsunami hit. He said he got through it by riding out wave after wave for almost an hour just holding onto his board for dear life. [5]

When the 8-magnitude earthquake struck on Wednesday morning, Chris was catching some waves on the south side of Savai'i island in Samoa with five other surfers.

He reported that all of a sudden, the water got super strange--something he hadn't ever seen before. It was like glass and got all lumpy and bumpy, and then started moving really fast, and he was getting sucked out to sea. He looked back at the shore, and the shore itself and got large being totally exposed above the water when a huge surge of water hit the shore.

He thought to himself, this is the end feeling he was going to be smashed into the reef or the forest jungle on the land. He and fellow surfers spent 45 minutes floating and timing the surges so they could ride them in without getting smashed.

Finally, once they were on land, they realized their surf camp was destroyed and all of their belongings washed away. Needless to say, all felt highly fortunate as the Tsunami tragically killed many in Samoa and neighboring American Samoa that very sad day in 2009.

**One Man's View of Getting Strong**. Arnold Schwarzenegger certainly achieved a great deal in his life being a World Champion Body Builder, a highly successful actor despite his Austrian accent "I'll be back", and a politician.

He's often said to get strong and built, your strength does not come from winning. It comes from struggling to develop strength. Going through rough times and maintaining a will to success is what he considers true strength.

**The Largest Fish Ever Caught Weighed Over a Ton**. So, there you were, minding your own business on a fishing trip in South Australia when suddenly your line went taut. At first, you think it's just another shark, no big deal. But as you start reeling it in, it becomes clear this is no ordinary catch. This thing is making your eyes almost pop out putting up one hell of a fight.

Well as you may know this actually happened in 1959, when Aussie Alfred Dean managed to wrangle in this aquatic behemoth, a whopping 2,664-pound great white shark, the largest fish reeled in recorded history! [6]

Just imagine trying to fit that in your freezer! Dean battled the shark for 50 minutes before it finally gave in, proving once and for all that everything in Australia is trying to kill you.

Dean's record catch dwarfs any other shark caught before or since. The next largest shark, a tiger shark, weighed in by a large margin of only 1,800 pounds. At the rate fishing records are broken these days, Dean's Monster shark should comfortably hold onto the title for a long, long time. Unless, of course, someone else hooks into a megalodon (a prehistoric fish -- the largest fish that ever known to exist), in which case we'll have bigger problems.

Any angler who manages to top Dean's mammoth shark deserves way more than just a footnote in the record books. They deserve their own Discovery Channel special. And probably hazard pay.

**Bizarre Marathon.** It was a hot and confusing summer day in Athens in 1896. The first modern Olympics were held there. The Marathon was chaotic. Many runners were suffering from the swirling heat and erratic exertion of the long and winding race.

Sam Mellor was somehow leading the disoriented pack but even he was experiencing severe and sporadic cramps. He slowed to an unsteady walk and eventually had to stop in a daze, unable to continue in the madness.

American runner Thomas Hicks was also strangely struggling in a befuddled way. At the unpredictable 10-mile mark, he came under the care of his two handlers in a frenzied fashion.

He plainly was in a big, muddled need to drink water in a frenzied manner, but they refused in a crazed way.

Instead, they gave him warm water to rinse his mouth in a wild fashion. They were trying to keep him hydrated without giving him too much liquid in his stomach in an unhinged manner.

Another American, Fred Lorz, was among those plagued by cramps in a deranged way. At the disoriented nine-mile mark, the pain was too much in a bewildered fashion, and he wanted to get a ride in one of the accompanying cars in a manic way and he did wave to spectators as he passed in a frenzied manner, hoping the car ride rest would allow his cramps to subside in an unbalanced way.

Seven miles from the finish in a befuddled fashion, Hicks' handlers gave him something more in a crazed way - a mixture of strychnine and egg whites. This was the first recorded use of a performance enhancing drug at the modern Olympics in an unhinged way.

Strychnine was commonly used as a stimulant in small doses. There were no rules against drugs yet in those bewildered times. His handlers also had some brandy but decided to wait before giving it to him in a deranged manner.

After his ride in a crazed way, Lorz emerged from the car feeling better. He got back on the course and continued running. One of Hicks' handlers tried to order Lorz off the course in a frenzied way, thinking he shouldn't be allowed to continue after getting a lift. But Lorz ignored him and kept going in a disoriented way. He finished in just under three hours. His handlers were befuddled.

The crowd went wild in a crazed fashion, believing an American had won. Alice Roosevelt, daughter of President Theodore Roosevelt, tried to place a wreath on Lorz's head and medal around his neck, but suddenly someone objected saying Lorz was an impostor since he got a ride in a car.

The cheers turned to boos as the celebration was halted. Lorz just smiled and said he was just joking! Can you believe it?

Meanwhile, the strychnine was taking effect on Hicks. He became pale and weak in a crazed fashion. When he heard Lorz was disqualified, he found new strength to keep going.

His handlers gave him more strychnine and brandy to help him continue. They washed his body with warm water, seeming to revive him briefly.

But the drugs were having a terrible and crazy impact and Hicks began hallucinating thinking the finish was still miles away. He begged for food and his handlers gave him more brandy and egg whites as he shuffled forward.

Finally crossing the line, they had to hold him up so his feet could move enough for him to be declared the winner. It took four doctors and an hour after finishing for Hicks to even feel well enough to leave. He had lost eight pounds during the grueling race. The drugs and hills had torn his body apart.

One year later, Hicks and Lorz would meet again at the Boston Marathon where Lorz was the true winner without any artificial aids.

**Catching a fish's eye.** If you enjoy snorkeling around reefs, check out the Cleaner Wrasse, a small fish that cleans other fish. It also responds to its own reflection in a mirror. So much so that it removes marks on itself when it sees them in a mirror which is one sign the fish is aware of itself.

Next time you're out fishing, use an eye-catching color since most fish are tetrachromatic (ability to see color vividly).

Cleaner Wrasse

## Sports/Events you may haven't heard of.

**Pillow Fighting - A Cushy Contact Sport.** Pillow fighting isn't just for slumber parties!

The Pillow Fight League (PFL) takes this childhood pastime to the next level with their semi-pro women's league. Founded in 2004 by Commissioners Stacey "Pillow Puncher" Case and Craig "The Cushion Crusher" Daniels, the PFL has brought the sport to Toronto and beyond.

Fights go down in legit arenas like they used to at that goth bars in Toronto. Cities like Montreal and even New York City have hosted bouts, but Toronto remains the pillow fighting capital.

Matches last just 5 minutes of feathery fluff flinging frenzy. If it goes the distance, three judges decide who wins. No leg drops or submissions allowed - just good old fashioned pillow pounding. Fighters can't grab each other's arms either. Referee sees that, it's a warning or DQ city.

While it looks like all fun and games, it's best to be cautious as pillow fighting is no joke. Fighters walk away with bruises! No biting, scratching or below the belt shots though -- instant ejection for that nonsense.

**The Running of the Reindeer** in Anchorage is part of their annual Fur Rondy fest. First held in 2008, it's like Pamplona but with caribou instead of bulls. Folks brave the Alaska cold to take on the charging herd down a downtown street. At least the reindeer are nicer than bulls!

**Cow Race Mayhem.** Cow racing is exactly what it sounds like -- a race with cows. The only place you'll find this madness is down under in Australia at the annual Compass Cup. These cows have zero training so it's total anarchy out there.

They pick 24 cows the morning of the race. Each one gets a rider and four "urgers" to try and keep them going straight. Spectators can even join in on the fun! The track is a measly 60 meters but over 5000 people pack in to watch the cows do their thing.

Some cows don't move an inch. Others spin in circles like ice skaters. A few mavericks go rogue and race in the opposite direction. Three heats narrow it down to the six craziest cows for the finals. Now that's entertainment!

**Underwater Smooching Showdown.** The World Kissing Competition in Italy takes kissing to the next level. Contestants compete in wild events like "basketball kissing" and the best one - underwater lock lips!

In the underwater round, pairs have to kiss at the bottom of a clear pool for as long as they can without coming up for air. Just imagining the bubbles and muffled moans has me in stitches. What a riot!

**Polish Dragon Boat Rumble**. In Poland they take dragon boat racing to the extreme with their version called "tug of oars" or "dragon war."

Teams of six to eight face off in boats, except instead of paddling in the same direction the teams face each other in one boat and go head-to-head, each side trying to muscle the other backward. A video of one such rumble in 2015 went viral and now more places are giving it a try - check out the YouTube referenced in the endnotes. [7]

Bring on the dragon boat rumbles! I'll grab some popcorn and watch the chaos unfold as they fight to the finish like gladiators on the high seas.

**The Paralympian's Stolen Dreams**. Paralympian Jen Lee had his hopes and dreams stolen in an instant. Jen is a 35-year-old Sled Hockey para-athlete who overcame immense challenges to earn three gold medals at the 2014, 2018, and the recent 2022 Beijing Winter Paralympics.

Through his military service and recovery from a tragic accident where he lost a leg, sport became his passion and helped give his life meaning.

Those medals represented so much - the years of grueling training, painful injuries, and lonely struggles that few could understand. But most of all, they symbolized the friends, coaches, and community that supported Jen every step of the way. Without them, his success would not have been possible.

Yet now, it was all gone in a moment and here is how the theft happened. As Jen left the parking garage last Saturday, he noticed a dark figure lurking in the shadows. His heart sank as the thief quickly smashed his window and grabbed Jen's backpack, containing the tangible trophies of his soul's journey.

When Jen reviewed the footage, he was overwhelmed with sadness. All his sacrifices swept away in an instant. He shared the video with the authorities.

Mercifully, his medals were returned anonymously the next day. The suspected thief was later arrested. The medals took on extra meaning for Jen after that unfortunate incident.

**What is sports success?** Stephen Curry often said, having success in sports isn't an accident. It's more of a choice you make. He of course believes confidence in sports is important and he's not afraid of anything when he's on the court. He admits he gets butterflied, nervous and anxious in big games, especially championship series games. He handles those as good signs that's he's ready for the moment -- it's what he's worked for.

**The Jockey Who Won a Race After Falling Off His Horse**. During a steeplechase race in New Zealand something very unusual occurred. A horse and a jockey, Des De Jeu and Aaron Kuru, took one of the most terrifying tumbles you have ever seen.

During one of the jumps, the horse completely lost his footing and fell flat on his side and stomach! And poor Aaron went tumbling out of the saddle!

Most thought for sure it was all over. But then, in a move that could only be described as pure daring and skill, Aaron somehow managed to hold onto the reins while the horse was on the ground!

And then, are you ready for this, he climbed back on while the horse was getting up! Can you even imagine keeping that kind of cool under pressure?! People were on the edge of their seats, just in awe of how he pulled that off. And get this - they didn't just survive the fall, they went on to win the race!

I mean, talk about defying the odds! That has to go down as one of the most amazing and gutsy performances by a jockey ever.

Thomas Edison once said, *"Many of life's failures are people who did not realize how close they were to success when they gave up."*

You have to see it to believe it and you can view the YouTube video of the race referenced in the endnote. [8]

Steeplechase racing

**The largest person to play in the NFL**. Aaron Gibson was born on September 27th, 1977, in Decatur, Illinois. He grew up loving both football and track and field. In high school, Gibson attended Decatur Central High School where he lettered in both sports. As a football player, Gibson held the impressive title of heaviest player in school history, weighing over 440 pounds during his high school career.

Gibson excelled on both sides of the ball. As a senior defensive tackle, he dominated with 8 fumble recoveries and 11 passes defensed, earning himself a spot on the prestigious First Team All-State team. College scouts took notice of Gibson's impressive size and skills, naming him one of the top 33 recruits in the state by the Bloomington Herald-Times.

Gibson chose to continue his football career at the University of Wisconsin. As a junior, he stepped into the starting role at right tackle, protecting Heisman Trophy winning running back Ron Dayne. Dayne went on to shatter the NCAA Division I career rushing record with 6,397 yards, thanks in large part to Gibson's blocking.

Gibson's senior season saw him cement his legacy as one of the best linemen to ever play for Wisconsin.

Following his dominant college career, Gibson's size and athleticism turned heads at the 1999 NFL Scouting Combine. Though clocking an impressive 40-yard dash time of 5.3 seconds at his massive 410-pound size, scouts saw Gibson's physical traits as the prototypical mold of an NFL right tackle. His "huge body with big legs and gigantic chest" gave teams confidence he could transition smoothly to the professional level.

**When a Marathon Runner Lost His Way and Still Won.** Victor Kiplangat of Uganda thought he had the Commonwealth Games marathon gold in the bag. As he approached the finish line in Birmingham, England, the streets were empty, and he had a huge lead. But little did he know, he was about to take a wrong turn for the ages.

As Victor turned down a side street, expecting to see the finish line banners waving in the distance, all he saw was a stray cat licking its paws. "Where's the finish?" he thought to himself, starting to panic.

The BBC commentary team were as shocked as anyone, as they noticed Victor looked more confused than a baby in a topless bar as he headed the wrong way from an aerial camera shot.

The TV footage showed the leader quickly turning back round after realizing his mistake, and looking a bit mad at himself continued and he still won the race!

The Ugandan's error was later well understood as most felt the course was a bit confusing and there should have been a lead bike.

**Tiny Strike Zone!** Eddie Gaedel was 3' 7" from the top of his head to sole on his foot and in 1951, he strolled up to the plate for the hapless St. Louis Browns against the Detroit Tigers. The Browns, led by legendary owner and practical joker Bill "Wild Bill" Veeck, were looking to give their meager fans a good laugh, and Eddie fit the bill — or rather, was the bill.

In a brilliantly madcap scheme, Veeck signed Eddie to an actual MLB contract and outfitted him in a jersey proudly displaying the uniform number 1/8. As the crowd roared with hysterics, little Eddie dug in against the Tiger hurler and, following orders to remain in his crouch, ambled to first on four pitches so wide they would've made Babe Ruth blush.

Eddie was promptly lifted for a pinch runner to a standing ovation from the howling horde. While the stunt raked in dough at the gate, Eddie walked away with a measly $100 for his efforts.

Sadly, the pint-sized pioneer's time in the show was cut tragically short when he was later pummeled by angry bowlers following a dispute at the bowling alley where he worked nights.

In a cruel twist, the only MLB rep at poor Eddie's funeral was the very pitcher who had unwittingly fueled the crowd's laughter by tossing him those four fat pitches.

Eddie Gaedel

**Wilt Chamberlain.** On the 2nd day of March in the year 1962, basketball legend Wilt Chamberlain scored an astounding one hundred points in a single game for the Philadelphia Warriors in their contest against the New York Knicks. This record stands as perhaps the most unbreakable in all of sports history, with only Kobe Bryant coming close to matching the feat some 44 years later in 2006 when he tallied a comparatively meager 81 points.

Wilt Chamberlain measuring an incredible 7 feet and 1 inch in height, possessing tremendous strength, and able to run and jump with such skill that he could have competed in the Olympic games, Wilt entered the NBA when the style of play was far slower than what we see today, with dunking being a rarity and many opting for the outdated two-handed set shot. Chamberlain revolutionized the game, often making his opponents appear as mere children before his dominance. In addition to his 100-point outburst in 1962, he averaged an astounding 50.4 points per contest over the entire season!

Sadly, as the contest was not televised, no footage exists of Chamberlain's historic night. Moreover, because the game took place in an alternate arena to the usual one, the mainstream press was not present to bear witness and provide documentation! It was not until the 1980s decade when the best evidence of this monumental achievement came to light - a reel-to-reel audio recording made by a fan of the fourth quarter radio call of the legendary game.

**The lightning match between tennis legends.** In the roaring twenties, Bill "The Master" Tilden dominated the courts like no other, cementing his place as perhaps the greatest server to ever swing a racket. Many egos fell before his shots, but none were vanquished so swiftly as the unlucky Brit known only as “D. Greig”.

When the stars aligned for a showdown between the United States and Great Britain prior to the prestigious grass court major at Wimbledon in 1927, Greig was tapped as a last-minute replacement for his countrymen. However, he would find no mercy facing the great Tilden in their opening bout.

Tilden tore through the first set in a blistering six games, and the second was no different. Greig did win two games in the third set, but Tilden prevailed in a mind-boggling twenty-two minutes of 6-0, 6-0, 6-2 dominance.

To this day, no best-of-five professional match has been completed in less time, cementing this lightning match as the shortest on record between tennis titans.

Bill Tilden

**Height is no problem**. Jack Emanuel "Soupy" Shapiro is the smallest person to play in the NFL. Standing 5 feet 1 inch, not many are familiar with him. He played just one NFL game in 1929, with the Staten Island Stapletons.

In the present day, Deuce Vaughn, a Cowboys rookie is 5 feet 4 inches and a talented running back. He's super-fast, and dashes, zigzags, cuts when you don't expect it, and exceptionally hard to tackle.

Deuce Vaughn

**Ever lose three clubs during a golf round?** We all have good days and bad days on the golf course. Champion golfer, Ben Crenshaw remarked, "My golf game's gone off so much that when I went fishing a couple of weeks ago my first cast missed the lake."

There was one professional golfer (with a record of 9 nine professional wins) who took losing his equipment to a whole new level. Dutchman, Joost Luiten, lost not one but three of his clubs up a tree at a tournament in Dubai.

Apparently, a few days earlier Rory McIlroy's tee shot landed in some fan's lap, which was pretty funny. On the other side of the coin, Mr. Luiten was frustrated after bogeying a hole and just chucked his driver into a tree. Bad move because it got stuck up there.

Then, trying to get it down, he threw another club at it. But that club eating tree with those thick branches just snagged that one too.

While some tournament official was climbing the tree and tossing sticks at the stuck clubs to no avail, Luiten kept trying to help by launching a third club at the tree. A few more throws and whaddya know, he was up to three clubs stuck in there.

Totally bizarre for Joost who has won six titles on the European Tour.

He even tried jumping and hitting the tree with a sign from one of the course helpers, but finally gave up. Had to finish that hole with only 11 clubs.

Many have said golf would be a boring game if it weren't for the ups and downs and mishaps.

Thankfully a volunteer eventually got the stuck ones down. Luiten ended up placing third from last in the championship.

Joost Luiten

**Outfielder arrested**. Back in 1983, the great Dave Winfield, a Hall of Famer, was the right fielder for the Yankees, and he was warming up before a game, throwing some balls around. Well, unfortunately one of his throws hit a seagull that was flying by, and it killed the poor bird.

This happened as well to 6' 10" Arizona pitcher Randy Johnson later in 2001 when he threw his well-known 100 mph (estimated) fastball and happened to hit a bird who unfortunately had chosen the wrong flight path resulting in an explosion of feathers!

The fans saw Dave hit the bird and they were not happy. They started throwing stuff out on the field, trying to hit Dave! Can you believe that? Well, the game went on but after it was over, the police showed up and actually arrested Dave! They charged him with cruelty to animals for hitting that seagull. Dave posted bail and in the end the charges got dropped.

The Yankees manager at the time was none other than Billy Martin who reportedly commented that Dave didn't hit that bird on purpose, and they would agree if they saw some of the throws, he'd been making all year!

Fast forward to 1994 now. The Minnesota Twins traded Dave to the Cleveland Indians for a player to be named later. The only thing was, after the trade there was a strike and the rest of the season got canceled.

Since there was no season, Dave never actually played for the Indians that year. And the Twins never did name the player they wanted in the trade.

A short while after that, some execs from the Indians and Twins got together for a fancy dinner. This place was 5-star, top of the line. And get this - the Indians execs picked up the whole tab! They later agreed that the cost of the dinner would be what they traded Dave for. Can you believe that? Dave became the only player in MLB history ever traded for a dinner.

Of course, age catches up to everyone, but Dave continued to achieve. These days Dave works as a special assistant for the MLB Players Association. He had an amazing career too being a 12-time All Star, a 7-time Gold Glove winner, a 6-time Silver Slugger, and more. And get this - in 2004 ESPN actually named him one of the best all-around athletes in any sport!

As far as Randy Johnson's accidental predicament went, Giants second baseman Jeff Kent came out of the dugout and carefully handled the bird and after pointing it toward Randy with a smile, took it back to the dugout.

Dave Winfield

**Unusual Pickleball Destination.** A highly elevated pickleball court is in Colorado at the Broadmoor's Cloud Camp. Sitting at a dizzying 9,200 feet above sea level, this Camp sits on Cheyenne Mountain and offers amazing views of Pike's Peak in the distance. But those vistas come at a cost -- you make an interesting journey to get there.

From May through October, pickleball adventure seekers can reach Cloud Camp by riding a mule. Now I've never actually seen a mule play pickleball, but getting one up to 9,200 feet seems to be an athletic feat in itself! Of course, you could also hike up the mountainside.

Your other option is to try driving an SUV up the treacherous slopes. Just make sure to pack a change of underwear -- those winding mountain dirt roads will have you white-knuckling the steering wheel.

After you finish the journey, you'll be rewarded with pickleball courts offering views that will take your breath away. Just try to get used to the different oxygen levels at that height as you hit a winning volley!

It may be tough to reach, but most say Cloud Camp is definitely worth it.

**Sports Quiz Question 2**. The national sport in Afghanistan is Buzkashi which is played by men riding horses and is similar to horse polo. But they don't use a plastic high-impact ball like the sport of polo. What do they use instead of a horse polo ball?

A. A ball of frozen cow dung.

B. A ball of frozen sheep dung.

C. A headless goat carcass

D. A compacted ball made of kidney beans, chickpeas and dhal (dhal is cooked lentils).

E. A ball of frozen noodles.

*Answer on p. 197*

**The Right Mental Attitude**. Michael Phelps is probably the greatest competitive swimmer of all time. He has said many times the way he handles competition is to know in his mind that he can only control his own performance. If he does the best he can, he feels good at the end of the day no matter what the outcome.

And he points out to keep in mind that it doesn't matter what else is going on. When you walk into the arena of competition for any sport, you focus on the task at hand and just do your best.

**The Referee Who Attacked the Player He was Supposed to Protect.** The job of a referee is to maintain order, enforce the rules, and protect the players in one of the toughest sports there is.

Sometimes, though, the refs get a little too into the action. During a hockey game between two Canadian high schools, one ref took "protecting the players" a bit too literally.

When a fight broke out, refs rushed in to break it up, as refs do. One official grabbed a player and dragged him away from the mele, possibly to issue a penalty or just get him out of harm's way. Unfortunately, the ref was so amped up that he decided the best way to "calm down" the player was by punching him in the face.

Not surprisingly, that didn't go over well with the player or his teammates who rushed in to defend their guy from the unhinged ref. Soon enough, the whole thing descended into chaos, the rest of the refs completely losing control of the situation they were supposed to be controlling.

The police had to be called in, and a couple of players earned suspensions, all thanks to one referee who got a little too hands-on. Check it out on the YouTube video referenced in the endnotes. [9]

Moral of the story: refs, stick to blowing the whistle and calling penalties. Let the players do the punching. Your job is hard enough without attacking the very people you're supposed to protect.

Sometimes players and fans frequently accuse refs of being blind. They may not be blind but usually have great self-control in an action-filled sport. Being a hockey referee isn't easy and those guys earn their money!

Hockey referees' work is exceptionally hard at a fast action sport.

## First American Downhill Olympic Champion.

William Dean Johnson achieved a well-deserved win and international fame and success when he won the gold medal in the downhill event at the 1984 Winter Olympics in Sarajevo, Yugoslavia (now known as Bosnia and Herzegovina). Something no American had ever done before.

For a very long time the Europeans usually win gold in the downhill and Austria leads all other countries in being awarded gold medals.

As the first American male to capture an Olympic gold medal in alpine skiing, and the first non-European athlete to triumph in the men's Olympic downhill, Johnson's victory cemented his place in sports history.

Johnson was born in 1964 in Boise, Idaho and learned to ski at a young age in the late 1960s at Bogus Basin near his hometown. In 1972, his family relocated to the Brightwood area just outside Mount Hood, Oregon, where Johnson honed his skiing talents on the slopes of Mount Hood.

He attended Sandy Union High School in Sandy, Oregon and in his teenage years struggled with behavioral issues that led to a run-in with law enforcement. To avoid serving six months in jail for his juvenile offense, Johnson was offered an alternative -- attending the renowned Mission Ridge ski academy in Washington state. He seized this opportunity to focus his energies on competitive skiing.

Johnson's raw talent was cultivated at Mission Ridge, and he went on to make the United States Ski Team. He made his World Cup debut in 1983, finishing a strong sixth in the downhill event in Austria. The following year, at just 23 years old, Johnson was poised to take on the European alpine skiing powers.

Some doubted the brash young American upstart, but Johnson embraced his image as a daredevil bad boy and was nicknamed "Billy the Kid".

He boldly proclaimed his confidence and love of fast living, stating he enjoyed driving over 100 miles per hour and getting airborne in his vehicle.

Johnson scored his first World Cup downhill victory in January 1984 on the storied Lauberhorn course in Switzerland, a breakthrough win as the first American male ever in World Cup downhill. He carried this momentum to the 1984 Winter Olympics in Sarajevo. Through strong training runs, Johnson showed he was well-suited for the course and predicted he would emerge victorious, drawing comparisons to iconic sports figures like Joe Namath and Muhammad Ali.

On February 15th, 1984, Johnson raced to the gold medal in a time of 1:45.9, beating silver medalist Peter Müller of Switzerland by 0.7 seconds.

With his Olympic gold, Johnson achieved international fame and established America's presence in alpine skiing's biggest competition. His victory story of natural talent cultivated through challenges and ultimate triumph against the odds serves as an inspiration.

William "Bill the Kid" Johnson

**Fastest Horses.** The greatest gallopers! Wow, these horses can really fly across the track.

The highest recorded race speed over two furlongs (1/4 mile) is an incredible 70.6 km/h, that's close to 44 mph! Winning Brew is considered to be the fastest horse and is in the Guiness Book of World Records for that amazing speed. [10]

Can you believe it? The speed record was set by an amazing horse named "Winning Brew" on May 14, 2008, at Penn National Racecourse. That's faster than Secretariat, Man O' War and Seabiscuit that are considered to be among the fastest horses ever.

Winning Brew is no ordinary horse, she's a champion and trained by the one of the best, Francis Vitale. This 2-year-old filly thoroughbred covered the quarter mile distance of 402 meters in a blistering fast time of just 20.7 seconds. That's flying!

To think a horse can run that fast over such a short distance is absolutely astonishing. But distance races require endurance as well as speed. And for longer races up to 1 1/2 miles, another champion emerged.

On October 14, 1989, at the prestigious Santa Anita Park in California, the 3-year-old "Hawkster" blazed to a record time of 2 minutes and 22 seconds for the 1 ½ -mile distance. Hawkster's average speed was a lightning quick 60.6 km/h -- roughly 38 mph!

So, in summary, Winning Brew and Hawkster showed what thoroughbreds are capable of on their record-setting days. There is a video on YouTube of Winning Brew to show you this horse in action referenced in the endnotes. [11]

The horse racing world is lucky to have seen such incredible athletic performances!

**Fan's snowball wrecks a Game-Winning Field Goal.** The legendary "Snowball Game" of 1985 lives on in NFL infamy. This epic clash between the mighty 49ers and high-flying Broncos was more than just your average regular season tilt - it was a blizzard battle for the ages!

As the snow swirled around frigid Mile High Stadium, John Elway and the Denver offense jumped out to an early lead. But the vaunted 49ers, led by cool customer Joe Montana, were just getting warmed up.

Just when it looked like San Fran would tie it up with a gimme field goal, all football hell broke loose. A barrage of snowballs rained down from the stands, thrown by drunken Denver fans still drunk from the night before. Mayhem ensued as poor Matt Cavanaugh was pelted from all angles. As snowballs bounced off his head like hailstones, the hapless holder bobbled the snap like a hot potato.

Panic seemed to set in as Cavanaugh scrambled to salvage the play. With snow still stuck in his eyes, he flung the ball blindly like a madman. Alas, his throw fell short as his receivers stood frozen in disbelief. The Broncos took over, cackling like the maniacal villains they were.

When asked about this comedic calamity, referee Jim Tunney could only shrug and say "What can ya do? There's nothing in the rulebook about snowball fights."

I guess mother nature had it out for the Niners that day. In the end, the real winners were the rowdy Denver fans, who helped deliver sweet victory through extreme measures. Their snowball barrage will forever live on in NFL lore as one of the greatest game-changing plays ever that wasn't actually a play. Truly a day to remember in the annals of pro football's frozen folklore!

In 2001, Green Bay police issued a warning backed by the Green Bay team before a game with the Cleveland Browns, that there is a city ordinance against throwing objects onto the field. The warning made it clear that if that should happen on a Sunday afternoon, it would result in immediate arrest and the Stadium would revoke the fan's season ticket. Nothing was thrown.

We all know fans in the stadium buy tickets, concessions, etc., and are important for NFL teams. In 2008, the NFL and all NFL clubs created and adopted a fan code of conduct. The NFL wants fans to enjoy the game experience but any fan who breaks the code of conduct will be ejected from the stadium with no refund and further prohibited from future games.

The code of conduct generally requires ejection, etc., if a fan(s),

- Has behavior that is unruly, or illegal in nature.
- Is intoxicated and acting irresponsibly.
- Uses foul language, obscene gestures and the like.
- Throws objects on the field or interferes with the game.
- Fails to follow instructions of stadium employees.
- Harasses the opposing team.

**The Basketball Player Who Scored for the Other Team in the Final Seconds.** An unfortunate high school basketball player had worked hard all season to help lead his high school basketball team to victory.

During the state championships, with less than 4 seconds left, his team was 1 point down and was inbounded the ball. He took off down the court like a rocket for what he thought was the game-winning layup.

An instant silence fell over the gym as both teams and fans alike processed what just happened. His teammates stood stunned on the court, unable to believe one of their best player had just messed up - as we all do in life.

As the imminent final buzzer sounded, the other team celebrated. The shame and embarrassment might just be too much to bear. But later, most everyone realized nobody's perfect and it's what you do after a mistake that defines who you are. In sports, competitors need to keep looking forward to better things.

Those are encouraging thoughts for this well-intentioned but unfortunate high school player who intended to save the day in the final seconds. Check it out in the YouTube referenced in the end notes. [12]

**Don't Give Up. Don't Ever Give Up**. One of the most inspiring speeches in sports was made by Jimmy Valvano, the legendary basketball coach. Dying of terminal cancer, he gave a highly emotional and motivating speech when he was awarded the Arthur Ashe Courage and Humanitarian Award.

He passed away about 2 months later. He was head coach at NC State and won the 1983 NCAA Division I men's basketball title against improbable odds favoring the Houston Cougars, in one of the greatest upsets ever in basketball history.

His speech is on YouTube if you want to check it out. [13]

**A Fearsome Defenseman Blossoms**. As you know, the Big Z, Zdeno Chára is a Slovak legend who dominated the NHL for over two decades! Standing tall at 6 foot 9 inches, "Big Z" was the most physically imposing presence to ever skate in the league. With his towering frame and fearless play, Chára cemented his status as the most intimidating defenseman of his generation and the tallest person ever to play in the NHL.

He likes to learn as much as he can and speaks many languages including Slovak, Czech, Polish, Russian, German, Swedish and of course English.

When he tore a ligament in his left knee in 2014 and couldn't travel with the team, he decided to take real estate courses and obtained a real estate license.

Big Z had never tasted Jello before coming to Canada to play hockey and didn't know what it was. He tried it when the folks he billeted with offered it to him.

Most writers who write stories about Big Z say he's a gentle giant off the ice.

Chára enjoyed immense success during his fourteen seasons captaining the Boston Bruins. He led the team with passion and skill, winning the prestigious Norris Trophy in 2009 as the league's best defenseman. Chára helped guide the Bruins all the way to Stanley Cup glory in 2011, cementing his place in franchise history. Few Europeans before him had achieved such heights in the NHL.

Remember those days with the Ottawa Senators when they had to choose between keeping the young Zdeno Chára or Wade Redden? How could they have known Chára would develop into an absolute legend? Even the New York Islanders who acquired him as part of a trade didn't realize they had a future star in their midst. But Chára was determined to prove everyone wrong, fueling his incredible rise to stardom.

With his towering 6'9 frame and 255 pounds of pure muscle, Chára was without a doubt the most physically imposing specimen the NHL had ever seen. But beneath the surface of his intimidating exterior lay a champion's heart. Chára played with a fiery chip on his shoulder, using his rare size and skill to dominate opponents into submission. It's no wonder he captured the coveted Norris Trophy, cementing his place among the league's all-time greats.

Opponents learned to truly fear Chára as he threw around even the biggest brutes with ease. Just ask Bryan McCabe - Chára made the 6'2 defenseman look like a child! And anybody who witnessed Chára's crushing hit on Max Pacioretty could ever forget it. The thunderous blow rang out across the league, only adding to Chára's legendary status as the most terrifying force in the game. Few mere mortals would ever dare to challenge this behemoth of the blue line!

Zdeno Chára was a one-of-a-kind titan who left an enduring mark on the NHL. His incredible career stands as a testament to what can be achieved through determination and hard work.

Chára's legend will live on forever in the annals of hockey history.

His general view of sports is that it's always a challenge and you go uphill at times and downhill at other times. You may have to take it slow sometimes, but always keep it going. He reported that it's tough for bigger guys to become agile and have quick feet and he kept training to increase agility. But through strong determination, confidence and hard work he did it exceptionally well.

Zdeno Chara

**61-Year-Old Wins the Sydney to Melbourne Ultramarathon.** This story is absolutely incredible! At 61 years old, Cliff Young showed everyone what determination and grit can do.

For almost 26 hours straight, this amazing man jogged an unbelievable 875km (that's over 543 miles!) from Sydney to Melbourne. Can you even imagine?

As he cruised into Melbourne in the late evening, the excitement was building. Even in the light drizzle, over 1,000 supporters had gathered, eagerly awaiting Young's arrival. They must have been on the edge of their seats, wondering how this legend would look after such an epic feat. And when he shuffled into view, though his expression didn't show it, you just know his heart had to be soaring at the incredible reception. What a moment that must have been!

At 61 years old, a potato farmer who chased cows around for exercise, Cliff Young was about to prove that age is just a number if you have heart.

Though he had a little more distance to go to the official finish line, it was clear Young had already cemented his place in the record books. Smashing the previous record by over 2 days, this amazing man was going to complete the course in an astonishing 5 days and 14 hours! And he wasn't even done yet -- he had 20 more km to go! You just knew everyone was in awe of what Cliff Young had pulled off.

With his nearest competitor 45km behind, it was obvious no one could touch Young on this run. And though others had briefly taken the lead, injuries and exhaustion caught up with them. But not Cliff - he just kept on going, mile after mile.

It was truly a classic story of the tortoise beating the hare. With simple tactics of avoiding burnout and maintaining his pace, Young showed what steady perseverance can achieve against more "experienced" competitors.

When he entered the race, surrounded by professionals with all their advanced training methods, I'm sure Young must have felt like a huge underdog. But he knew himself and his abilities best. By tossing out schedules and charts, and simply running without long rests, he found a way to win when no one expected it.

What an inspiration! From Sydney all the way to Melbourne, just putting one foot in front of the other through sheer will power.

What a well-deserved victory and $10,000 purse for this true champion. He showed the world that day what the human spirit is capable of. An absolutely incredible story of triumph against all odds. Cliff Young, you are a legend!

**Baseball's Rube Waddell's Crazy Antics on and Off the Field.** Rube Waddell was one of the greatest pitchers of his time, but he also lived life to the fullest. Born just outside Bradford, England in 1876 as George Edward Waddell, by the time he reached the majors in 1897 he went by the nickname "Rube".

Rube played in Major League Baseball for 13 seasons and had an incredible earned run pitching average of 2.6 while striking out an astonishing 2,316 batters across five teams, including two years with the Pittsburgh Pirates.

His best years came with the Philadelphia Athletics from 1902 to 1905. There, Rube won 97 games and baseball's pitching triple crown, leading the league in strikeouts.

He played his final major league game in 1910 before passing away from tuberculosis at the young age of 37. He's a player in the Baseball Hall of Fame, being inducted in 1946.

Besides being a highly talented pitcher, he was one of the most entertaining and enjoyable athletes to ever play the game.

Even during games, Rube did his own thing. He was known to play marbles with kids under the stands while his teammates searched for their starting pitcher. His wild antics earned him a unique salary - he was paid his $2,200 yearly wages in single dollar bills because of his impulsive spending.

Rube would also ask his manager if he could pitch both games of a doubleheader, just so he could sneak off fishing for a couple days afterwards before his next start.

Rube loved animals. At spring training in Jacksonville, you could find him wrestling alligators for fun. He also had a strange attraction to fire trucks and would sometimes chase after them, causing his teammates to assign someone to make sure Rube made it to the ballpark.

While talented, Rube's hijinks didn't always make him popular in the clubhouse. He got into many verbal spats with teammates and managers over his off-field adventures. Rube's most famous fight was supposedly with teammate Andy Coakley over a straw hat, resulting in a shoulder injury that caused Rube to miss the 1905 World Series. Some thought the fight and injury were staged so Rube could avoid throwing in the Series, perhaps to bet against his own team.

Alcohol was at the heart of many of Rube's antics. He struggled with drinking problems, earning the nickname "sousepaw" from reporters. Rube couldn't even remember how many times he had been married due to his drinking. This landed him in legal trouble for bigamy at one point. In 1903, Rube was even arrested during a game for assaulting a fan who criticized his pitching. In 1910 he passed out drunk during a game and that ended his career.

He was a great pitcher. He struck out a record 302 batters in 1903 and 349 the next year.

In 1905, Rube won a pitching triple crown with 27 wins, 287 strikeouts and a 1.8 ERA. His talent and success earned the respect of even his toughest critics. Rube's tombstone epitaph, paid for by his former teammates, reads simply - "Rube Waddell had only one priority, to have a good time."

Rube Waddell

**The 1904 Olympic Marathon: Chaos From Start to Finish.** That 1904 Olympics in St. Louis sure was an unusual event! Being tied to the World's Fair certainly added an interesting flair.

While there were some amazing performances, like the gymnast with a wooden leg winning multiple gold medals, overall, it seemed more like a sideshow than the prestigious competition we think of today.

The marathon in particular really highlighted how unconventional things were. They had experienced marathoners in the field but also all sorts of "oddities" like barefoot tribesmen and a former mailman from Cuba who had to hitchhike part of the way after losing his money gambling!

The conditions for the marathon itself sounded incredibly tough. Over 90-degree heat, dusty roads, hills, traffic to dodge -- it's amazing anyone finished!

They only had two water stops too, which seems crazy now. During the race one man nearly bled to death from stomach issues caused by all the dust. Wild dogs chased one another!

That mailman from Cuba, Felix Carbajal, was a real character. He kept stopping to chat and even snatched some peaches from a car when refused one! Unfortunately, he later got sick from rotten apples he ate while running.

What a wild event that 1904 marathon in St. Louis was. It's easy to see why the Olympics organizers almost scrapped the whole thing after that spectacle!

**An unusual place to play tennis.** Did you know there is a one-of-a-kind tennis club in New York City? It's called the New York City Vanderbilt Tennis Club. Conveniently located and open to the public inside Grand Central Terminal, 4th floor. The address is 15 Vanderbilt Avenue - 4th Floor, NY 10017. [14]

*New York City Vanderbilt Tennis Club*

**The Case of the Course Croucher.** In the quiet Norwegian town of Hafrsfjord in 1984, Stavanger Golf Club's head greenskeeper came forward with a harrowing tale of terror on the links. A mysterious mad man had been targeting holes on the course, leaving massive mud monkeys that no lady lurker could possibly lay.

Grounds Superintendent Ole Olson said dookie discoveries dated back to 2005 but had ramped up of late. "He's got a couple holes on speed dial," chuckled Ole. "And we know it ain't no frail fanny dropping such dumps -- these turds are too tremendous to be from a woman!"

Ole noted the defecator only struck on weekdays, mysteriously missing weekends. "I've never found so much as a nugget on the course come Saturday or Sunday," pondered the perplexed poop police. Clues like used toilet paper taunting taped to trees led Ole to deduce a deranged defecator was on the loose.

Club Director Steinar Floisvik shed some light, revealing bicycle tracks at the scene of the crime. "In the dewy dawn, I spied pedal prints on the putting green. Footsteps showed where business had been boomed, and the bike tracks backtracked the same sad path," shared Steinar solemnly.

Fellow groundskeeper Geir tried to deter the dastardly dumper by installing high intensity spotlights but found them dismantled the next day! "I couldn't believe my eyes but sure enough, he'd climbed a tree and crawled out a limb to disconnect the lights. How he avoided electrocution or plummeting is beyond me," gasped Geir.

To this day, the motive of the mysterious mad man making monstrous mud monkeys on the course remains a mystery. The greenskeepers can only guess he hates golf or lost his marbles.

**Sky high baseballs.** Babe Ruth was known for his fun-loving personality both on and off the field. In July of 1926, he participated in quite a publicity stunt for the military training camps. As part of the event, Ruth attempted to catch a ball that was dropped from an airplane flying about 300 feet above Mitchel Field on Long Island. Donning an army uniform for the occasion, Ruth gave it his best shot. It took him seven tries but he was finally able to snag the ball out of the sky.

The New York Times covered the story. They reported on how hot and dusty it was that day. The Babe was darting all over the place under the scorching sun. It was getting hotter by the minute and the circling airplane at 300 feet kicked up more dust that swirled in tiny tornados of dust around the baseball legend.

After Ruth's caught the seventh ball dropped, all congratulated him, and some newspaper reports even suggested Babe should be put in charge of catching bomb drops from an attacking enemy.

A few other notable high flying ball catches include one by Chicago Cubs catcher Gabby Hartnett on April 1st, 1930. On that day in Los Angeles, a ball was dropped from a Goodyear blimp estimated to be flying around 800 feet above the city.

Then in 1938, Cleveland Indians catchers Frankie Pytlak and Hank Helf each snagged balls thrown from the top of Cleveland's 708-foot-high Terminal Tower.

**Small rod big fish story**. This fisherman is the epitome of never say die attitude. For example, there is a story about a fisherman spotting a mammoth 807-pound blue marlin off the coast of the island of Madeira. He could have used larger gear, but chose a light tackle rod and reel with only 20 lb. line! Most people would have thought it was impossible, but not this guy. He was ready for the challenge.

It took him over 70 minutes which must have felt like an eternity as he battled against all odds to reel it in. What an incredible achievement. You can just tell this fisherman has nerves of steel and never knows when to quit. Even in the face of what seemed like insurmountable adversity, he persevered. What an inspiration.

The details of how it all went down are so exciting. Seeing that massive fish swimming so close, yet having to make a perfect cast with the light tackle - the pressure must have been immense! And then the marlin took the bait. I can't imagine the adrenaline pumping as the fight of his life began. How lucky that the fish stayed up near the surface where he had a chance, instead of diving deep. This guy's luck was definitely in that day. Think about those leaping acrobatics and keeping the boat in position through it all. What a nail-biting ordeal!

This fisherman's epic triumph of the underdog is one for the ages. His incredible skills, grit and determination in the face of the ultimate challenge will be remembered and admired for years to come. He is a true hero and the ultimate example that nothing is impossible if you really believe in yourself and never give up!

**Small rod small fish story**. Wow, can you believe how small these fish are?! Catching tiny fish in Japan takes some serious skills. They've perfected the art of Tanago fishing over hundreds of years - catching fish that are smaller than a coin! Now that's what I call precision.

The smaller the fish, the bigger the achievement. They don't just go after any old small fry - these fishermen are aiming for the ultimate tiny catch: a fish that fits perfectly on a one-yen coin. We're talking micro-sized here, people! A fish that's barely larger than a dime. Can you even see something that small on your line? These guys must have eyes like a hawk.

Using handcrafted bamboo rods and ultra-fine thread under a microscope - the precision and patience required is unbelievable. While the rest of us are reeling in the big ones, these talented anglers are perfecting the art of the miniature catch. If net-fishing the tiniest fish was easy, it wouldn't be such a celebrated skill. But navigating tiny rods and lines that are huge compared to your quarry - now that's a real challenge! Check out the YouTube video of Tanago fishing referenced in the end notes. [15]

**The World's Fastest Pitch -- so far.** The Guinness Book of World Records reports the fastest pitch ever thrown was recorded at 105.8 mph (170.2686 km/h).

Aroldis Chapman threw that fireball when playing for the Cincinnati Reds in a game against the San Diego Padres, in San Diego, in September 2010. The pitch speed was measured by Statcast which is a high-speed, extremely accurate, automated tool developed to analyze player movements and athletic abilities in Major League Baseball.

Others argue there were faster pitches such as Bob Feller at 107.6 mph at Griffiths Stadium. [16] Or Steve Dalkowski's 110 mph pitch was the fastest. [17] But those gentlemen, who many considered to be the fastest pitches in baseball did not have modern technology to detect the actual speed when they were active so those reported speeds aren't recognized.

Aroldis Chapman

**"Nobody beats Vitas Gerulaitis 17 times in a row."** When Gerulaitis and Connors met in the 1980 Masters semi-finals, it was clear the crowd was feelin' Jimmy C. While Vitas V had impressed with his gritty comeback win over Lil' Johnny Mac in the round-robin, beatin' the talented lefty in a real doozy, his record against Connors told a different story. Those in the know about men's tennis were aware Connors had Gerulaitis' number on the speed dial. Their previous meetings always ended the same - with Jimmy breakin' out the bubbly to celebrate another win.

Headin' into their semi-final showdown, Gerulaitis had taken an unreal 16 straight L's against Connors. Sixteen losses in a row to the same dude is no laughing matter. The stats didn't lie -- Connors knew Vitas' order and how to deliver it. But Gerulaitis was never short on confidence. Deep down he believed he could flip the script, even if the bookies and fans thought otherwise. It was gonna be an uphill battle for Gerulaitis to snap his long losin' streak against his nemesis Connors and advance to the Masters final. Only an inspired performance could defy the odds.

It was shapin' up to be another W for Jimmy Connors early in the first set against Vitas Gerulaitis. Connors jumped out to a 5-3 lead and found himself with a set point in the ninth game. However, this game got really confusing thanks to multiple overrules by the line judges. After Gerulaitis saved the first set point, Connors earned another. Incredibly, Gerulaitis saved that one too with an ace that was initially called out but was actually in. As Gerulaitis served his second serve, Connors showed sportsmanship and merely pushed the ball back towards Gerulaitis and walked to the deuce side, signalin' he was awardin' the point to his opponent.

Gerulaitis was surprised by Connors' gesture, but managed to return the ball. Due to all the mistakes and uncertainty caused by the line judges in that game, Gerulaitis hadn't even realized it reached set point. After the match, when asked about it in his presser, Gerulaitis said "Was that set point? I think he knew the ball was an ace and he gave me the point. Connors would later explain that he grew tired of all the confusion caused by the officials during that game. He got caught in the middle and simply wanted to be fair to Gerulaitis.

Unfortunately for Connors, his display of good sportsmanship did not help him take the set. Gerulaitis took the next four games to snag the first set 7-5. He rode that momentum to break Connors' serve twice in the second, winnin' it 6-2. In his own press conference after the match, Gerulaitis had a memorable quote for the history books when he said, "And let that be a lesson to everyone: nobody beats Vitas Gerulaitis 17 times in a row."

**Sports Quiz Question 3**. On June 24, 2000, Mike Tyson knocked out Louis Savarese after only 38 seconds in the first round. Announcer John Gray of Showtime interviewed Mike shortly after the quick match ended. During that interview, Mike called out to another boxer shouting, "I want your heart, I want to eat your children…" Who was the fighter that Mike was calling out to fight in him in his next match?

A. Francois Botha

B. Tyson Fury

C. Lennox Lewis

D. Wladimir Klitschko

E. Chris Bird

*Answer on p. 198*

**Muhammad Ali's Great Grandad was an Irishman.** Ali's great-grandfather, Abe Grady, was an Irishman that settled in Kentucky in the middle of the 19th century. He married a freed slave. Their granddaughter was a lady named Odessa Lee Grady Clay who gave birth to the great boxer. Ali certainly has the gift of the gab.

He learned how to box at the age of 12. That happened when he went into a police station to report his red and white Schwinn bike had been stolen and the officer, Joe Martin, who happened to be a boxing trainer suggested he should learn how to box. He joined a gym and soon thereafter he won his first boxing match. Six years later he won the Olympic Gold Medal in boxing at the 1960 Olympics.

Many regard him as the greatest heavyweight boxer of all time. He had amazing speed as a heavy weight and if you've never seen him "Float like a butterfly, sting like a bee" or the "Ali Shuffle" there is a YouTube of his amazing speed referenced in the endnotes. [18]

Muhammad Ali

**A Soccer Team's Lead Executive Punches Referee**. Play was suspended league-wide after a leading club official of the team attacked a referee.

In a shocking turn of events, Faruk "Mad Dog" Koca, president of the notorious Ankaragücü club, decided the referee had made too many bad calls.

It was a scene right out of the movie "Raging Bull". Halil Umut Meler, a respected referee with accreditation to officiate international matches was hit with a devastating overhand right delivered from Farook who rushed onto the field to get Halil.

Meler crashed to the turf, seeing stars bigger than the ones on the Turkish flag. When the dust settled, Halil emerged from the battle with a shiner the size of a grapefruit.

The club's president, Faruk, was later arrested by local authorities. In other words, he lost his cool and his marbles after this sad event.

The "Night of Fisticuffs" as it's now being called had the Turkish football world in an uproar. Faruk Koca has been banned for life but claimed he was simply defending his team's honor after a string of questionable calls.

The league will try to move on but the black eye left on face of the referee may take some time to heal.

The referee eventually made it to the dressing room with the help of the police, who had to fight through the angry mob who were also after him in order to rescue the fallen referee.

Since the incident, Koca has resigned as club president. He apologized to the Turkish refereeing community, the sports public and everyone in Turkey.

Like that makes up for leaving Meler looking like one of the creatures from a low budget sci-fi flick! Apologies only go so far when you've put someone's life in danger.

Faruk was also involved in politics but after that event, his political career came to a halt.

**Most consecutive gold medals - Durable athletes**. It's often been said that it's tougher to stay on top than it is getting there. The Indian hockey team won the Gold medals in six consecutive Summer Olympics starting in 1928, 32, 36, 46, 48, and 52. It is the only country to have won gold medals in 6 consecutive Summer Olympics. Amazing as that is, it was a team effort.

Individually, Steven Geoffrey Redgrave CBE DL, one of the greatest British rowers of all time, won gold medals at five consecutive Olympic Games from 1984 to 2000 and is considered to be the most successful male rower in Olympic history. He is the only athlete ever to win five successive Olympic gold medals in an individual event.

There are six athletes who have won gold medals in 4 consecutive Olympic Games. They are,

- Paul Elvstrøm of Denmark, 1948–1960 in Sailing.
- Al Oerter of the US, 1956–1968 in Discus.
- Carl Lewis of the US, 1984–1996 in the Long Jump.
- Kaori Icho a lady from Japan in free style Wrestling 58/63 kg.
- Of course, Michael Phelps of the United States, 2004–2016 Swimming, 200 m individual medley

- Mijaín López of Cuba, 2008–2020, Wrestling - Greco-Roman 120/130 kg

Winston Churchill once said, "Success is walking from failure to failure with no loss of enthusiasm." We all know these amazing athletes, like anyone else, experienced failures yet despite it all they endured and delivered their best performance every 4 years as far as they possibly could.

Sir Stephen Redgrave

**World record – Fastest Serves!** Wow! Did you hear about the absolutely insane tennis serve that went down a few years ago?! Sam Groth, an Aussie player, registered the fastest serve ever during a tournament in Busan, South Korea.

We're talking 163 mph, which converts to a little over 262 kph! Can you even imagine hitting a tennis ball that freakin' fast?! I'd be terrified I was gonna give someone a black eye in the stands!

Unfortunately for Sam, as amazing as that record-breaking smokeball serve was, it wasn't enough to pull off a win that day. He lost that second-round match 3-6, 4-6 to a guy from Belarus. It really goes to show that while power and speed are awesome, you still gotta have the all-around game to come out on top.

But you have to respect Sam Groth for unleashing that monster serve and securing his place in the history books. The next guys coming for that record are gonna have to really step it up if they want to top 163 mph. At that speed it's difficult for the human eye to track it! What an absolutely insane athletic feat - Sam Groth is a legend whether he won that match or not! [19]

As for the ladies, you won't believe the power and speed of Sabine Lisicki's serve! She absolutely crushed the ball with her power to record the fastest serve ever seen in women's tennis. Lisicki proved all the doubters wrong who say women can't serve fast when she fired off a serve clocked at an incredible 210 km/h (130 mph)!

Can you imagine hitting a ball that fast over the net?! She must have some crazy strong arms to generate that type of velocity.

Sabine Lisicki has cemented her name in the history books with that record-breaking serve. She showed the world that day that women can also dominate on the court with pure athleticism and strength. [20]

But hold on. Another woman pro, Georgina Garcia Pérez absolutely crushed a serve at the 2018 Hungarian Ladies Open that clocked in at an insane 220 km/h (136 mph)! That speed is just unreal for a tennis serve.

In the final round of the tournament, Georgina must have been feeling herself. It must have been an absolute blur and then a huge crack as the ball exploded off her racket.

To be able to serve that fast with pinpoint accuracy is truly remarkable. No doubt it played a huge role in helping Georgina win the match and take home the title at the Hungarian Ladies Open. [21]

## Soccer players under the spell of witch doctors.

It seems the soccer stars of Africa just can't get enough of those wacky witch doctors! Former the Republic of Côte d'Ivoire player Gilles Yapi Yapo says he was led down a merry path of sacrifice and debt tunes of $200 grand by a traditional healer. He said he got under the witchdoctor's spell, and it messes with your head.

Yapi Yapo was going through some rough times with his old club Nantes when his uncle badly suggested a visit to a Parisian potion slinger. Yapi Yapo reported that witch doctors enjoy a high status in the Republic of Côte d'Ivoire. But this shaman had some doozy demands like sacrificing cocks, goats and, of course, cash to undo supposed "curses".

When the witch doctor tried to get him to sacrifice his own kid, Yapi Yapo knew it was time to vamoose. Yapi Yapo had been with the witch doctor two years and $200 grand lighter, our guy was through playing voodoo victim.

Another Ivorian import, Cisse Baratte, also got hooked by hoodoo back in his soccer days. He started with magic potion showers and sacrifices, wearing a do-rag with Koran verses sewn in for luck. Dressing rooms were full of players wearing perfumes and talismans from Senegal and Cameroon.

The recent brouhaha around French star Paul Pogba proved witchery in soccer is still going strong. Pogba's own brother and friend claimed he paid a witch doctor to hex teammate Kylian Mbappe!

Pogba and the hoodoo man denied the doozy deal, but it tends to show even the best players in the world can't resist having a little hexing on the other guys as long as it helps them.

**Superstitions and Other Things About Aaron Judge**. Did you know that Aaron Judge was adopted and didn't even know it until he was around 10 years old?! "They picked me out and chose me to be part of their family."

How amazing is that? And get this - he still calls and talks to his adoptive parents every single day. That's so great they have a wonderful relationship.

Did you also know that Aaron was a 3-sport star athlete in high school at Linden High School in California? He played baseball, basketball, and football! And get this - he still holds the record at his high school for career receiving touchdowns in football.

When asked why he chose baseball in the end, Aaron said he liked the chess match between the pitcher and batter. It makes it a thinking game and he loved that. No wonder he's so good at hitting, with that kind of mind for the game!

Here's a fun little superstition Aaron has - right before the first pitch, he pops two pieces of sugar-free Dubble Bubble gum in his mouth. Then he chews them until he makes an out! Can you imagine how nasty that gum must get if the game goes on for a while?

Did you know Aaron wears the number 99 but that he actually prefers number 35, which was worn by his hero Reggie Jackson? Unfortunately, that number is retired now. Maybe one day the Yankees will let him switch!

Even though as a star athlete he was offered college scholarships from powerhouse schools like Stanford, UCLA and Notre Dame, Aaron chose to play ball for California State University, Fresno - where his parents went! How cool is that to follow in their footsteps?

It's just incredible to think that even after being drafted by the Oakland A's right out of high school, Aaron still went to college for three more years of ball at Fresno before the Yankees drafted him number one overall in 2013. Talk about dedication to the game and bettering himself as a player!

Now in Yankee Stadium, the right field bleachers used to just be for regular fans but now there are 18 special seats called "The Judge's Chambers" - because let's face it, Aaron towers over everyone! And they even dress up the fans in those seats in wigs and robes to make it look like a courtroom.

With Aaron standing at an enormous 6'7", you just know there have to be lots of hilarious jokes made about his height. I just love imagining him joking around in the batter's box like "I think I feel a raindrop, is it starting to rain?" and the poor catcher looking up at him like "no way, the sky is clear!" Only for Aaron to respond, "Well it's still falling, it'll hit you any minute now!" Aaron seems like such a funny and lighthearted guy. What an amazing baseball star!

Aaron Judge

**Sports is Real.** Travis Rice in 2013 was considered to be one of the best snowboarders in the world by many sportswriters. He pointed out sports is very real and gets you away from the everywhere digital world we live in. Instead of clicking for things, sports makes you do it yourself physically and you just get out and do it.

Watching sports inspires many people to go out and do the best they can. Famous baseball player, Jackie Robinson recognized that when he said, "Life is not a spectator sport. Don't spend your time just watching. Go out and do it."

**Big Bowling**. Wow! check out this epic bowling center! The absolutely massive Inazawa Grand Bowl in Pearl City, Japan holds the title of the world's largest bowling alley. We're talking over 91,000 square feet of lanes with no pillars to get in the way - just pure bowling bliss stretching as far as the eye can see!

When you factor in the total floor space, this place is a whopping 182,000 square feet. It truly is an architectural marvel. Oh, and did I mention it has 696 lanes ready for bowlers to unleash their skills? I can't even imagine that many players all bowling at once.

The best part is when you ride that escalator up you are greeted by the most spectacular view. That is, as soon as you reach the top, BAM - you see all 116 lanes in their fully lit up glory.

It must be a bowler's dream to roll those balls down such an immense stretch of polished hardwood. This place is bowling nirvana and definitely deserves its title as the world's most massive bowling fun factory. Inazawa Grand Bowl is one of the coolest sports venues on the planet!

Inazawa Bowling Centre

**Did you know how fish detect movement?** (You probably already know this) "Fish have sensory scales along their body called the lateral line. These sensory scales can pick up low-frequency sound waves that vibrate through the water. So, it makes a lot of sense to drop an anchor as quietly as possible.

Also, salmon are known as one of nature's best navigators due to their sensory capabilities. As most know, salmon know the way back to the same river they were born in order to spawn. They amazingly use their own guidance of magnetic fields and their sense of smell detecting pheromones that are unique to their home stream." [22]

Salmon swimming upstream.

**Infamous Butt Fumble**. The year 2012 was truly a dark time for the New York Jets - let's be real, it had been a dark two decades. But little did they know, things were about to get a whole lot darker. . and funnier.

On Thanksgiving Day, 2015 as the Jets faced off against their hated rivals the New England Patriots, Jets quarterback Mark "Butterfingers" Sanchez was about to provide the most comedic Thanksgiving gift this side of a frozen turkey.

On 1st and 10, Sanchez took the snap and immediately went full-on slapstick, botching a hand-off so badly that in his scramble to salvage the doomed play, he slid face-first directly into the backside of his own offensive lineman Brandon "Big Butt" Moore.

The crowd howled with laughter as the ball popped out like a bar of soap, right into the waiting arms of the Patriots for an easy touchdown.

Thanks for the gifts, Butt--erfingers! The Jets would never live this one down. You can see it happen on the YouTube referenced in the endnotes. [23]

**Michael Jordan didn't make the cut trying out for Varsity HS Basketball.** Can you believe it? The GOAT, Michael Jordan, didn't make the cut while trying out for the high school varsity basketball team!

It's absolutely insane to think that MJ, the man who led the legendary Chicago Bulls to six NBA championships, didn't make the varsity team as a sophomore.

Born in Brooklyn in 1963, MJ and his family later moved to North Carolina where his older brother Larry fueled his passion for the game. But standing at just 5'10 as a sophomore, the HS coach chose another friend of MJ's who was a towering 6'7" for the final varsity spot.

You can imagine how devastated MJ must have been! But as the old saying goes once you take a hard fall you turn that into a high bounce so long as you're made of the right material.

He wasn't going to give up. He simply got more determined to show everyone what he was made of. Every morning before class, you'd find MJ in the gym putting in that work. Over the summer he grew over 6 inches and made the varsity team as a junior, scoring 35 points in his first game!

From there, we all know the incredible career that followed - 6 championships, 6 Finals MVPs, and countless other records.

And get this - in his entire career, MJ scored in double digits in every. single game except one, where he played just 16 minutes recovering from an injury!

So, while H.S. Varsity's coach's decision was a major setback at the time, it lit a fire in MJ and fueled his path to becoming one of the greatest of all time.

Just goes to show that with hard work and determination, you can overcome anything!

Michael Jordan

**The Great One**. This guy was born to play hockey, growing up on his very own backyard rink in Brantford, Ontario. Now even though he wasn't the biggest guy out there at only 6 feet and around 180 pounds, don't let that fool you because Gretzky had so much heart, smarts and skills on the ice.

With his endurance, instincts and agility, it was like he could see into the future to know exactly where that puck was going to end up. And he had the innate ability to dodge checks coming his way while the other guys were zooming around like their lives depended on it to grab the golden puck.

Not only does Gretzky hold the record for the most goals ever with 894, but even if you took all those away, he would still be the leading scorer with a mind blowing 1963 assists!

Can you believe that assist total?! It just goes to show that Wayne was always looking to set up his teammates instead of just focusing on himself. He wasn't afraid to take or shot or pass for an assist at any time.

You know what they say - keep your mind open and your passion for learning alive. And you'll never hit a goal or an assist if you don't aim for it, so take your best shots out there! The rewards are waiting for those willing to give it their all.

As Gretzky himself said, "Hockey is the best because you need every single guy on your team pulling together and helping each other out to succeed. What an amazing team player he was, and what an inspiration "The Great One" continues to be!

Wayne Gretzky

**Sports Quiz Question 4.** What is the oldest sport(s) in sport history?

A. Archery

B. Swimming

C. Wrestling

D. Chariot racing

E. Weightlifting

F. Running

G. C and D.

H. A and B.

I. None of the above.

*Answer on p. 199*

**Phil Mickleson is actually right-handed.** If you're right-handed, did you ever try to do things left-handed? Just plain awkward for many!

Little did young Phil know as he swung his first club just how difficult golf would become. Mirroring his father's left-handed swing seemed natural at the time. Only years later would Phil discover just how unique his style truly was.

While other kids his age were developing their games using their dominant hands, Phil forged ahead left-handed. Every shot, every swing presented a new challenge that right-handed golf simply didn't offer. Gripping the club was only the beginning - controlling distance, direction, and spin went against his natural instincts.

But Phil didn't know any other way. This was how his father hit the ball, so this is how he would learn too. Through trials and errors on the practice range, Phil slowly mastered the left-handed swing. It was a struggle at times, like trying to hold eating utensils in your opposite hands that you're used to. But Phil's determination and love for the game drove him forward.

Now, decades later, Phil has proven that playing against the grain can pay off. As one of the most successful left-handed golfers ever, he has shown it is possible to find an unconventional path to the top. Phil Mickelson is living proof that with enough practice and perseverance, even unnatural abilities can be honed into a unique gift.

On the lighter side, David Feherty said an anecdote that (here's a brief excerpt), *"Phil is brilliant, but he's nuts. There's something not quite right about that boy. Phil is watching a movie that only Phil can see.*

*"His mother told me, 'Phil was so clumsy as a little boy, we had to put a football helmet on him until he was 4 because he kept bumping into things.'*

*"I told her, 'Mary, Mary, I'm a writer, you can't keep handing me material like this.'*

*"So, the next time I saw Phil I said, 'You didn't really wear a football helmet in the house until you were 4, did you?' He said, 'It was more like 5.'"*

Phil Mickleson

**The unusual sport of Phone Throwing**. Do you have some old cellphones lying around your home, ready to be tossed in the trash? Well hold onto those bad boys because they could be your ticket to sporting glory! Just do like those crazy Finns and turn those outdated devices into the next big thing - Phone Throwing.

You heard me right, folks. Phone Throwing is an actual international sport that originated in the year 2000 in Finland of all places. I'm guessing things get pretty boring up there during those long winter nights.

The rules? Simple as can be - just wind up and chuck that mobile as far as your arm can throw. Style points are awarded, so put some zip on it! Judges will measure the distance and critique your form.

The current world record is held by Dries Fereman. Can you believe he launched his old Nokia clear across 110 feet? That's farther than what most people throw anything!

Instead of ditching that dusty drawer-dwelling device, consider giving it a new lease on life. Strap on those athletic shorts, stretch out those throwing muscles, and get ready to hurl your high-tech hunk-of-junk into sporting history.

Winding up for a phone throw

**The unique sport they call Bossaball**. Now I've heard of regular old football, volleyball, and soccer. But have you ever in your wildest dreams heard of a sport that combines all three of these into one insane mashup?

Introducing the craziest new game on the planet - bossaball!

It's like someone said "You know what these sports really need? Trampolines! And gymnastics flips!

Some play it inside a giant bouncy ball?" Because that's exactly what bossaball is. Take the best parts of soccer, volleyball, and football and throw it all in a blender on steroids. Bam! You've got bossaball!

Can you imagine trying to score goals, set, spike, and pass all while bouncing around like a lunatic? The coordination and athleticism you'd need is off the charts. You'd better bring your A-game cause these players are no joke. I'm talking muscles upon muscles, flips, spins, the whole nine yards. Try keeping your cool while ricocheting off the walls like a pinball.

If you're looking for the most insane, adrenaline-pumping, sure-to-cause-whiplash sport out there, bossaball is calling your name. No more of this standing around business - it's all action all the time with bossaball. The only thing sweating will be from laughing your butt off at the three-ring circus before you.

Get your game face on and get bouncing! Check out the bossaball YouTube video referenced in the endnotes. [24]

**Fast Question**. What did the bad soccer announcer get for Christmas?

COOOOOOOOOOAAAAAAAAAAAAAAAAAAAAAAA
ALLLLLLLLLLLLLLLLLLLLL!!!!!!!!!!!!!!!!!!!!!

**Who needs both hands?** Jim Abbott was born without a right hand. Can you believe that? But that didn't let it get him down. He went to the University of Michigan and totally dominated.

In 1988 the big leagues came callin'. He got drafted in the first round by an MLB team. And get this - after just one year in the minors he was called up to the show. Can you imagine overcoming something like that and making it to the major leagues? What a story!

He liked baseball and wound up playing in the Major Leagues for the Angels, Yankees, White Sox, and Brewers, from 1989 to 1999. [25]

You wouldn't think a one-handed pitcher could throw a no-hitter but when he was with the Yankees, he threw a no-hitter against the Cleveland Indians in 1993.

He felt the no-hitter was the highlight of his career and very special. Many people ask him about it, and he usually responds how fortunate he was that no batter was able to hit a drop-in looper somewhere. Jim is a popular motivational speaker now.

Jim Abbott

**The Ancient Sport of Shin Kicking**. From the shadows of history emerges a competition so bizarre and brutal that it seems more fiction than fact. Shin kicking, a contest lost to the mists of time, has survived into modern days on the fringes of society.

Two warriors of iron will, and flesh stand before one another, eyes locked in a primal challenge. In this moment there are no rules, no mercy -- only the clash of bone and sinew as kicks are unleashed with relentless fury.

The thud of impacts echo across the field, a savage symphony that strikes fear in any onlooker. These are no mere athletes but gladiators testing their limits of endurance and courage.

Blood may flow, yet still they fight on through waves of agony. Such is the heart and dedication required to compete in this most extreme of sports.

Though civilized lands have outlawed its barbarism, a secret society keeps the tradition alive through underground tournaments.

In the hidden arena of Cotswold Olimpicks, near Chipping Campden, England in the spring, the World Shin Kickin' Championships are held each year. [26]

Scouts scout far and wide for those few possessed of the indomitable spirit to challenge the pain. It certainly takes a lot of endurance to be the last man standing and crowned champion amidst a landscape of fallen foes.

If the call of battle sings in your veins, come witness history's wildest spectacle - but beware, for in shin kicking the line between spectator and participant can blur in an instant.

Destiny awaits those bold enough to answer its call into the arena of bones. Check out the sport on YouTube in the link referenced in the endnotes. [27]

**Choosing**. A disgruntled and neglected wife says to her soccer crazy husband, "Choose, either me or the soccer game!"

The husband replies, "Give me 90 minutes to think."

**Unicycle hockey?** Have you ever gazed up at the stars and dreamed of soaring through the cosmos on but a single wheel, battling opponents with stick in hand and balance as your co-pilot? Well, your visions have now become reality!

Unicycle hockey is no mere pastime. It is an intergalactic odyssey of dexterity and daring the likes of which this world has never seen.

Stepping onto the courts is to embark on a journey where land and sky collide. Players ride not mere unicycles but vessels of wonder, propelling themselves forward with nary but a pedal's push.

In hand they clutch not mere sticks but scepters of skill, with which to guide the orange orb of fate. And when opponents collide in a clash of wheel and will, it is to witness the stuff of legends -- man and machine merging in a display of coordination beyond imagination.

To join their ranks demands mastery not only of balance but balance in motion. Feints and fakes must flow as fluidly as the tides, for a moment's hesitation means tumbling from your celestial steed.

The quick turns of a viper, the vision of a hawk -- such talents you must possess to outmaneuver your foes. And through it all the orange orb demands your focus, your touch as light as down yet as sure as the rising sun.

So, will you answer the call? Will you mount your unicycle steed and take to the courts of the skies? The tournament awaits those brave enough to defy gravity with grace alone. Your place in the annals of greatness is there for the taking, if only you dare. What say you -- will unicycle hockey be the stuff of your legend? The choice, dear friend, is yours.

There are unicycle hockey leagues and clubs in Australia, Germany, Switzerland, the UK, France Denmark, Sweden, Hong Kong, Taiwan, and Korea. [28] There is also international competitions. [29]

Unicycle hockey

**MMA Fighter's Pants Sag in the Octagon.** There have been many tall tales told in the MMA community over the years. One story that has taken on a life of its own is the legend of Tim "The Training Pants" Sylvia's unscheduled bowel movement during a televised bout. While long considered an urban myth, Sylvia has now come clean about the poop fiasco.

"I don't want to take anything away from my opponent Assuerio, he may be a tough dude, but I was clearly full of something else that night. A few good shots landed but I just couldn't seal the deal. What can I say, I ate something funny and spent the whole fight holding in a massive mudslide.

"Between warmups in the freezing room and going back and forth outside, I definitely caught a bug. By fight time, all bets were off keeping Hershey squirts at bay. If you look close during the match, you can see when my shorts start to sag that there's more than sweat stains in the undies."

Thankfully for Assuerio, it was punches not pinches that ended our battle in the bathroom.

Sylvia pulled off the win despite the extra cargo, narrowly avoiding giving new meaning to a "head leg scissors and arm takedown" finish. Some things are better left in the toilet, not the highlight reel.

**Amazing Canadian lady wins cheese rolling despite being knocked out!** This is a bit hard to believe but it's true and shows how incredibly determined and tough these cheese rollers are!

A woman was knocked completely unconscious while racing down the steep hill after the cheese, but still managed to win! She was a Canadian lady named Delaney Irving!

What an amazing achievement! After taking a nasty fall and being knocked out cold, she didn't even remember winning the women's race! She only found out when she woke up in the medical tent. Talk about tough as nails! But she said it was all worth it to take home that cheese-y gold. The footage of her fall is on YouTube and it's wild to see and is referenced in the endnotes. [30]

One moment she's racing full speed, the next she's tumbling head over heels down the slope. Scary stuff! But like a true athlete, she shook it off and still powered through to claim that first place title. Her determination and grit is super inspiring.

The men's races were just as intense! First place winner Matt Crolla from Manchester did say you've got to be very brave or a little bit crazy to go down that super steep hill and do something that nuts.

With competitors traveling from as far as the US, Canada, Japan and Switzerland, you know this race is a big deal. It puts little Brockworth, UK on the map as a destination for adrenaline junkies and cheese lovers worldwide. What an awesome tradition that keeps drawing in crowds year after year. Three cheers for these amazing cheese rolling champions!

**Gym etiquette.** A bearded older man approached a young attractive woman who was focusing and concentrating hard on her weightlifting exercises. He stood politely nearby and waited for her to finish her set before attempting to get her attention.

After she finished, she noticed him for the first time. The older man, in a gentle tone showing he did not want to disturb her doing her workout, said, "Excuse me".

She ignores him.

He waits a bit then repeats "Excuse me" a little louder.

She stops with an annoyed look on her face as she takes out her earphones and stares at him and says, "I have a boyfriend."

He replies, “So do I. Here’s your cell phone that you left on that machine.”

The gym brings all kinds of people together, and though misunderstandings can occur, staying friendly and giving others the benefit of the doubt usually makes it a welcoming place for all to better themselves in body and spirit.

**Extreme Ironing - The most adventurous household chore ever!** Can you believe there's actually a sport that combines the thrill of danger with the excitement of getting out wrinkles? Extreme Ironing has taken the world by storm! We're talking about strapping an ironing board to your back and tackling ironing in some truly epic locations.

Rock climbing with an iron in hand? Bungee jumping with a steam press? How about skydiving with a portable clothes steamer! You better believe it - these extreme ironing athletes are taking household chores to insane new heights. Literally! We're talking pressing shirts at 30,000 feet in the air or getting those creases out from atop a towering mountain peak.

Can you even imagine the adrenaline of taming wrinkles at such death-defying altitudes? The concentration it must take to get shirts smooth as a baby's bottom while your life is on the line. It's absolutely nuts!

These extreme ironing enthusiasts live for that perfect press no matter what crazy obstacles they have to overcome. They'll go to the ends of the Earth to beat out those pesky wrinkles - and have the time of their lives doing it!

Extreme Ironing

If you would like to see more totally insane versions of sport like extreme ironing (e.g., underwater on the sea bottom, biking, snowboarding, waterskiing, etc.), check out the YouTube referenced in the endnotes. [31]

**Father and Son get record trout!** Scott Enloe and his son Hunter were in for the catch of a lifetime while out on beautiful Blue Mesa Reservoir in Colorado.

The action started immediately. Hunter reeled in a massive 31-pound lake trout for a great start. But they had their sight set even higher. Their goal was to break the 50-pound barrier and possibly set a new state record.

Using his high-tech depth finder, Scott spotted something truly jaw-dropping under the surface. At first, he thought it was a group of large 30 pounders, but then he saw it - a giant purple, teal and black blob unlike anything ever seen. Hunter was skeptical it was two fish, but Scott somehow had the feeling from his experience this was one singular beast.

The epic battle was on! For 13 minutes Scott fought valiantly to bring in a colossal 73-pound trout. But for Scott, there was a higher purpose. After confirming its size, he swiftly released the legendary leviathan back into the reservoir.

Why? To respect this ancient survivor and preserve the magic of Blue Mesa for generations to come.

Releasing it without weighing it on land means it won't be an official record. But that moment will live on forever in Scott and Hunter's memories of their wildest fishing adventure ever. An experience they will relive and cherish for decades to come.

The largest trout ever? Possibly. But its impact goes far beyond any record or trophy. It's a reminder of the simple joys and timeless wonders still found in our natural world.

The IGFA, however, is all about catch and release and conservation of our amazing fish species. While some states still have outdated rules, the IGFA knows what's up -- record fish deserve to live another day.

For world records, the IGFA makes sure every fish is weighed the same way on solid ground, so the measurements are super accurate. But more importantly, they want anglers to safely unhook fish and get them back in the water ASAP. Weighing on land is just to cross all the t's and dot all the i's.

And they're working hard with other groups to convince more states to adopt humane practices. Last year over two-thirds of world record catches under the IGFA were released unharmed.

Catching a record fish is about the thrill of the fight, not just getting a number on the board.

**One of Rugby's Greatest**. A young man was on his "OE" (overseas experience) after university graduation exploring deep, remote jungles in the Amazon inhabited by tribes who still follow ancient ways.

Struggling his way through dense jungle, he was surprised by a few tribal warriors who, out of nowhere, suddenly leaped out at him waving spears and clubs. Fortunately, one of the natives spoke a little English and asked where he was from.

"New Zealand," said the young explorer.

“Nuu Zeeelund?” asked the puzzled tribesman.

"Jonah Lomu?” the young man suggested.

“OOOH! JONAH LOMU! Yeah! Yeah!”

Jonah Lomu was simply unmatched on the rugby field. Around 6' 5" (1.95 meters) and 265 pounds, he had the rare combination of power, size and lightning speed that made him almost unstoppable when he carried the ball. He ran the 100 metres in under 10.8 seconds.

He'd run faking would be tacklers to left, to the right, then barrel straight over them. Can you imagine seeing this huge mass of athletes sprinting at full speed at you?

It's no surprise then that Jonah scored in every World Cup match and the only rugby player ever featured on the cover of TIME magazine.

Even McDonald's and Madame Tussauds wax museum recognized how unique and influential he was!

While he may have lacked money growing up, Jonah more than made up for it with his incredible natural talents. He was born in South Auckland to Tongan parents and began playing rugby with no shoes, and still outran every kid at athletics meets.

Just ask rugby fans about Jonah Lomu and watch their eyes light up as they excitedly tell you "You couldn’t stop him! He was unstoppable!"

New Zealand is rightfully proud to call Jonah one of their own. Mentioning his name is all it takes to spark enthusiasm and national pride in any Kiwi. At the age of 19, he was the youngest person ever to become and play as an All Black - the National Team of New Zealand.

A humble, gentle natured man with passion for sports, he was known throughout the world and used his celebrity status to support the less fortunate in South Auckland and other charities such as UNICEF. He often paid bills for his childhood friends.

You know, not giving up is often misunderstood. People think it just means doing the same thing again and again, hoping for a different result. But true grit is about being willing to try different things when what you're doing isn't working. It's about having an open mind to new possibilities.

Take Jonah for example. His goal was to be the best rugby player he could be. But it didn't happen overnight. There were certainly times when his usual training routine wasn't cutting it anymore. That's when his real strength of character showed. He was willing to switch things up, try new techniques or strategies until he found an approach that helped him succeed.

His message is that true grit is a flexible thing. It's not about blindly plowing ahead the same way when you're stuck. It's about having the courage to adapt, to try new approaches, to keep evolving until you find your path forward.

There's Jonah Lomu jokes too. He loved playing against England and beating them. As the half-time whistle blew, the All Blacks led England 50 - 0, with Jonah getting eight tries. The rest of the team decided to head for the pub instead of playing the second half, leaving Jonah to go out on his own in the second half.

After the game Jonah walked into the pub where he told his teammates the final score: 95-3.

"What!!!! How did you let them get three points??!"

Jonah replied "Sorry, I didn't play the last 20 minutes." ☺

Check out the two YouTube videos in the end notes showing this huge great man in action . [32] He was so hard to stop. [33]

Jonah Lomu

**The longest shot**. The size of a basketball court in the NBA is 94 feet long and 50 feet wide. So, what's the longest shot ever in a basketball game?

The NBA doesn't keep records of the longest shot. Most say Baron Davis made the longest shot when he was playing against the Bucs and made about a 90-footer with 0.7 seconds remaining in the third quarter. You can see two videos of the shot on YouTube at the two links shown in the references. [34]

Baron Davis

The Guinness World Record is for the longest basketball shot by anyone not in a game (i.e. making attempt after attempt) was made by Joshua Walker in 2022. [35] After several tries, Joshua sunk a shot from 113 feet and six inches away.

The longest shot ever made blindfolded was 73 feet 10 inches by Harlem Globetrotter, Ant Atkinson. That is truly amazing!

**Cabbage under the baseball cap.** Babe Ruth had a piece of cabbage under his hat which he changed every two innings to keep him cool. Mr. Ruth stood 6'2" and weighed 215 pounds and the cabbage helped in those days to keep the head cool.

Babe currently has the record according to the Guinness World Records for the longest home run hit in a Major League Baseball game. His shot went flying and travelling 575 ft. against the Tigers in Detroit in 1921.

There was another blast reported by Guiness World Records of Mickey Mantle's home run that purportedly went 634 feet in a 1960 game against Detroit in the same stadium. However, further research revealed the newspaper's reports of Mickey's huge homer apparently was erroneous and there were distance miscalculations. [36]

When he hit the record homer, Babe was playing against his hated rival Ty Cobb. He was playing at his physical peak at the age of 26. Winds were about 20 mph blowing straight out to center field.

Manager-player Ty Cobb told his pitchers not to give Babe anything good to hit and Babe kept getting walked until he came to bat in the 8th inning and hit the first pitch over a wall and the wall itself was 560 feet from the plate in center field.

**Ball in play -- live action time**. According to researchers, the average Major League baseball game takes about 3 hours and ten minutes, and there is only about 18 minutes of live action. [37]

The average National Football League game takes about 3 hours and 10 minutes and there is only about 15 - 20 minutes of live action.

The average National Basketball game takes about 2 hours and there is only about 48 minutes of live action.

The average National Hockey League game takes about 2 hours 20 minutes and there is only about 60 minutes of live action.

The average soccer game takes about 1 hour and 55 minutes and there is only about 58 minutes of live action.

The average time for four players to play a round of golf riding in an electric cart without being delayed by the group in front of them is from 3 to 3 ½ hours.

The average time without a cart is about 4 hours.

Live times for a golf ball's flight, rolling, chip, pitch, putting, etc. has (as far as we can tell) hasn't been scientifically studied yet but it is probably less time than buying beverages from the attractive lady who operates the drinks cart on the course.

**Strange Olympic Event in 1900**. The 1900 summer Olympics were held in Paris. One of the events (and it's since been banned from Olympic competition) was a live pigeon shooting competition.

300 pigeons were released into the sky above the competitors, and they took aim.

Leon de Lunden a Belgium sportsman won the gold medal by shooting down twenty-one of the 300 birds released. [38] Hopefully most of the birds flew away.

Leon de Lunden

**He's a legend.** Do you love professional wrestling? Pro wrestling may be totally fake, but many enjoy watching it for the extreme athleticism and entertainment value involved in the performances.

As the star Bobby "the Brain" Heenan said, "I am a legend in this sport. If you don't believe me, ask me."

**Motorsport -- The Ferrari**. Ferrari holds the record for the most Formula One Grand Prix victories with 243 and McClaren holds second with 183 wins.

Ferrari's performance started off well then slumped a bit. Ferrari really started turning around in the mid-1970s thanks to this driver Niki Lauda. His skills behind the wheel helped Ferrari win the drivers' title in 1975 and 1977.

Around that time, other drivers like Jody Scheckter and Gilles Villeneuve also found success, helping Ferrari win more titles. Ferrari had another good period in the 1980s when they won the Constructors' Championship in 1982 and 1983.

After some less successful years in the 1980s and 1990s, Ferrari had a great run in the 2000s mostly because of Michael Schumacher. He joined the team in 1996 and helped them win five straight drivers' titles from 2000 to 2004. They also won six straight constructors' titles starting in 1999. Especially in 2004, Ferrari was super dominant and only lost a few races.

Even after Schumacher left, Ferrari still had some success - Kimi Raikkonen won the drivers' title in 2007 and they won the constructors' title in 2007 and 2008.

In 2023, Red Bull Racing dominated with Ferrari and Red Bull Honda following. Max Verstappen is Red Bull's top driver and comes from a racing family. Max's dad, Jos "The Boss" Verstappen used to race in Formula One back in the day. He was even teammates with Michael Schumacher at Benetton! Jos raced in F1 for eight years and finished on the podium twice.

Although Jos is most known for a crazy pit fire accident, he had at Hockenheim in 1994 - Jos had a miraculous escape from it. Max's mom Sophie Kumpen was also a professional driver! She used to race in the lower leagues against drivers like Jenson Button, Giancarlo Fisichella and even a young Christian Horner.

You might not have heard this one. A young man buys a brand-new Ferrari Roma Spider. He's all excited driving it home when he stops at a red light. Next to him pulls up this old timer on a little yellow moped.

The old man looks over at the Ferrari and goes "Hey Sonny, what kind of ride is that?"

The young guy replies "It's a Ferrari Roma Spider! I always wanted one since I was a kid. Set me back over $300,000!"

"Whoa, that's a lot of dough!" says the old timer as he tugs on his suspenders. "Why's it cost so much?"

"Cause this baby can do up to 200 miles an hour!" brags the kid.

The moped man asks to take a peek inside. "No problem" says the kid. So, the old man sticks his head in and checks out all the flashy buttons and lights. Sitting back on his moped he says, "Nice ride kid but I'll stick to my moped!"

Just then the light changes. The kid wants to show the old timer what his Ferrari can do. Floors it and bam, hits 100 mph in no time. Then he sees something yellow in his mirror, getting closer fast! Slows down and wouldn't you know - the moped blows right past him!

Kid's like "What the heck?" Pushes the Ferrari to 120 mph. Up ahead he sees the moped again! Kicks it up to 150 but the moped passes him again. Now he's confused. Gives it all she's got until nearly 200 mph. But sure enough, here comes the moped bearing down on him again!

Ferrari's redlining, nothing left. All of a sudden, the moped plows right into the back! Kid jumps out, can you believe the old dude's still kicking. He runs up "Anything I can do?"

The old timer wheezes "Unhook... my... suspenders... from... your... side view..." Then passes out.

Ferrari Roma Spider

## The first Olympics -- What were the events?

The first time the Olympic Games were held was in Greece in 776 BC. There weren't many events. Actually, just one. It was a barefoot 200-meter dash footrace. The person who won the first Olympic race was a man named Koroibos.

Koroibos didn't win anything. He was a simple cook by trade. Similar to many athletes in history, he thanked Zeus (his Deity) for his victory.

The five Olympic rings in modern day represent continents with colors signifying as follows,

Blue -- Europe

Yellow -- Asia

Black -- Africa

Green -- Australia

Red -- Americas

The interlocking of the rings mean a unified international world of equals and they also represent the core values of the Olympic spirit, excellence, friendship and respect.

The Olympic creed is meant to show it's not at all about winning. It is along the lines that winning is not important. The crucial thing is not to win but to have competed and fought well.

**Did you see that shot?!** A few hockey players have absolutely rocketed pucks at amazing speeds. The fastest shot and the World Record was set in 2012 by a superstar in the KHL League (fka Russian Superleague) named Aleksandr Ryazantsev when he absolutely torched a slap shot at an incredible 114. 27 mph. No typo, that's over 100 miles per hour! According to officials, it was the hardest shot ever seen.

While the KHL recognizes this record, the NHL has questioned it since the distance to the goal is shorter in KHL games. But still, talk about a howitzer!

Previously, the record was held by Denis Kulyash who blasted one at an astounding 110 mph back in 2011. Seems no goalie has a chance to track and block those missiles!

And five-time NHL Hardest Shot winner Zdeno Chara unleashed a rocket at the NHL All-Star skills competition that clocked in at a blistering 108 mph. That set the official NHL record and shows that even the biggest guys can really slap the puck like a canon!

What were the original hockey pucks like? They used to make the first hockey pucks out of frozen cow manure and leather liver pads. Can you believe that? No wonder they only lasted one game though, they'd get all soft again after hitting the ice a few times. I don't think anyone wanted to keep putting cow crap back on the ice. After that didn't work out too well, they started using wooden pucks instead.

Over time, folks started calling pucks "biscuits" too. Can't say I'd want to eat one if it was made from cow poop or wood! The players also used to say they were going to "put the biscuit in the basket" when they scored a goal.

Nowadays in the NHL, all the pucks get frozen before each game. That helps them slide better on the ice and bounce around less. Makes the game a lot smoother and more enjoyable to watch compared to back in the early days with those flying cow manure objects!

Ever wonder about rink ice thickness? The ice layer in a professional hockey rink is only ¾ inches (1.90 cm) thick and kept at -9°C (16°F).

The reason for keeping the ice layer thin is because it allows the water to freeze faster and harder. The thicker the ice, the softer it becomes and slower it freezes.

The Stanley Cup Hockey Championships are one of the most amazing tradition in sports! Can you believe that each player on the winning team gets to take home the Cup for a day during the summer? Talk about the ultimate prize! And the things these guys do while enjoying the Cup are unique.

The Stanley Cup

For example, Blackhawks' Andrew Desjardins loves Lucky Charms, so he filled the cup up with the magically delicious cereal. You know he was in heaven chowing down straight from Lord Stanley's Mug!

- Tampa's Mathieu Joseph treated himself to a hearty helping of Canadian poutine right in the Cup. You gotta respect a guy who mixes up fries, gravy and cheese curds like that.

- -Slovakian legend Marian Hossa took the Cup pierogi party to a whole new level, eating from it three times as a Blackhawk.

- LA's Tyler Toffoli used it as an ice cream bowl!

- When Tampa Bay won in '04, Nolan Pratt filled 'er up with puppy chow for his good boys. Now that's sharing and celebrating in style!

- Kings great Luc Robitaille dug into his favorite meatballs straight from the silver platter. Beauty goal, my friend!

- Blackhawks sniper Patrick "Kaner" Kane satisfied his buffalo wing craving right in the Cup. Nice!

- LA's Alec Martinez had it filled with M&Ms and took it on a bar crawl to share the glory.

**The Stanley Family**. The entire Stanley family was dedicated to growing the game of hockey. In 1915, the leagues worked together so their championship teams could face off every year for the ultimate prize - the one and only Stanley Cup!

The Stanley family promoted the game. In 1915, the National Hockey Association (NHA) and the Pacific Coast Hockey Association (PCHA), which were the two main professional ice hockey organizations. Their respective championship teams played each other every year for the Stanley Cup.

It's official name is Dominion Hockey Challenge Cup. It's become known as the Stanley Cup since it's named after Lord Stanley, the Governor General of Canada, who donated it as an award to Canada's top-ranking amateur ice hockey club. [39]

Lord Stanley

**Fight For Your Dreams!** Wow, what an inspiration MLB pitcher "El Culichi" is! His real name is Julio Urias and he's truly legendary.

Can you believe he had to have three eye surgeries as a kid to remove a mass which almost made him blind in his left eye?

But he didn't let that stop him -- as he says, the Lord gave him a good left arm to make up for it.

You've gotta love the tattoo on his neck -- "Always fight for your dreams and never give up!" That's his motto for sure. He's the best in the business at picking runners off base, with an incredible 6 pickoffs last season.

Many of us have dreams or goals we work on. Julio didn't give up and kept dragging himself forward with all that he had. It wasn't always fun or easy, he just kept going.

It's a wonderful feeling of accomplishment to push yourself past what you think your limits are. It's like proving yourself wrong and finding out you've got more courage and strength than you thought. It shows how your mind can trick you into thinking you're done when you've still got way more fight left in you.

When pitching, Julio guns it at 90-95 mph regularly, once even hitting an insane 97 mph. But it's not just speed, his changeup is dirty at 80 mph too.

In August alone last year, over 18 innings he only gave up ONE run total. And he led his team to wins against some powerhouse teams like the Giants, Twins, and Brewers.

With an awesome 0.0 ERA and 34 strikeouts in 30 innings, it's safe to say this guy gets the job done. You'll never see him back down from a challenge. He's not the kind to give up, that's for sure.

In the 2022 season, he finished 17–7 with 166 strikeouts and led the National League in ERA with 2.16.

Julio "El Culichi" Urias

**Ski Dubai?** Can you believe Ski Dubai makes that possible?! They have 25,000 square meters of indoor slopes, lifts and runs all under one huge dome in the middle of the Mall of the Emirates.

They even built an indoor tennis court inside the ski resort. How wild is that? Maria Sharapova and Lindsay Davenport battling it out in the snow, preparing for a tennis tournament in Dubai. I mean, Sharapova is from Siberia, so she's used to the cold, but she even said playing among the artificial snowfall was "surreal". What an incredible facility to bring winter sports to the desert. It's truly amazing.

**World Record for the Fastest Volleyball Serve**. Nimir Abdel-Aziz set a new record for the men's fastest serve with a blistering service speed of 137 km/h.

However, a few days later, Wilfredo Leon broke that record in European Volleyball one km faster at 138 km/h or about 86 mph!

**Okay buddy, put 'em up and let's get ready to rumble for the next 7 hours!** Andy Bowen and Jack Burke sure knew how to go the distance back in 1893. Those guys fought for an insane 110 rounds over the course of 7 hours and 19 minutes.

Each round was 3 minutes, but they just kept going and going. When they hit the 108th round, the ref John Duffy had seen enough. He told the fighters that if there wasn't a knockout in the next two rounds, he would call it a draw.

Neither guy could muster up a finishing blow, so Duffy declared it a no contest. At that point, who could blame him?

By the end, both Andy and Jack were so tired they couldn't even leave their corners. I mean Jack broke both his hands during the fight and needed two weeks of bed rest after! That's very understandable when you've finished punching someone for over 7 hours straight.

Those guys definitely hold the record for longest fight but there are some other extreme boxing stats too. According to Guinness World Records, the fastest knockout ever was only 4 seconds after the bell started ringing. That happened in 1947 at a Golden Gloves tournament in Minneapolis. Mike Collins clocked Pat Brownson, and it was lights out instantly. Can't get much quicker than that!

The shortest world title bout lasted a mere 20 seconds in a fight in 1993 in Puerto Rico. Gerald McClellan knocked out Jay Bell to win the WBC middleweight belt. McClellan must have caught Bell with a perfect punch right off the opening bell.

**An Old Winter Olympic Sport!** Olympic figure skating dates all the way back to 1908 in London. The history of figure skating goes back even further.

The earliest ice skates have been found and carbon dated back to 3000 BC! They were made from horse, ox and deer bones, then were strapped to the feet with leather. And they used a metal spike pole to push themselves across the ice.

In 1572 iron was used to make skate blades. The new metal blade skates made their way to North America with Scottish immigrants.

In 2014, Ari-Pekka Nieminen from Finland set the ice-skating speed record. This rocket man flew across the ice at an extraordinary speed of 156.4 kph and he set that record in Norway.

And the fastest speed on rollerblades is held by American hero Arne Kitze who took it to another level in 2007 blasting past the old record at a new record speed of 222.9 kph (138.129 miles per hour)!

**Novak the Amazing Polyglot!** The English word "Tennis" has such an interesting history, coming from the Anglo-Norman term "Tenez. Isn't that wild?

It's called "tenis" in Spanish, "tenisas" in Lithuanian, "ithenisi" in Zulu, "wangqui" in Chinese, "tenisi" in Samoan, and "tenisu" in Japanese. But get this - in almost every language around the world, the word for tennis sounds remarkably similar! How cool is that?

Serbian tennis star Novak Djokovic is the most multi-lingual athlete you will ever meet! He can speak an incredible 11 different languages. 11!!! Can you even imagine knowing that many? The languages are Serbian, English, French, Chinese, German, Italian, Spanish, Arabic, Russian, Portuguese, and Japanese. I mean,

Wow! That is enough linguistic knowledge for him to communicate with around 80% of people on the entire planet. 80%!

Novak is truly one of a kind - a total wordsmith and champion on the court. What an achievement! Check it out on YouTube referenced in the endnotes. [40]

**Sports Quiz Question 5.** Getting in shape. What is the World Record for the longest time in a forearm plank position?

A. 2 hours 49 minutes 11 seconds

B. 4 hours 5 minutes 34 seconds

C. 82 hours 1 minute 32 seconds

D. 9 hours 38 minutes 47 seconds.

*Answer on p. 199*

**The Doggy That Saved the Day**. In Argentina, a beautiful canine came out of nowhere and stopped a sure goal during a crucial soccer match, becoming an overnight internet sensation and capturing the hearts and belly rubs of fans worldwide. The hilarious hijinks showed that sports can always be ruff and the lighter side of competition is sometimes just a good boy away.

This incredible moment occurred when some striker from the opposing team booted the ball towards the net just as the goalie was going to kick it downfield. The striker kicked, but just as it looked like chow time for the other team, an unknown dog appeared and made one amazing save for an animal blocking the ball and leaving everyone in the stadium, from players to pooch lovers, howling with laughter.

The video of the heroic hound's goal-thwarting went viral faster than you can say "who's a good boy" as fans everywhere barked their praise at the pup's impeccable timing and impressive reflexes -- the YouTube video is referenced in the end notes [41].

It just goes to show, sometimes all you need is a dog with a nose for the ball to steal the show!

**The Longest Pickleball Rally EVER!** Can you believe this incredible record set in this amazing sport? Guinness World Records shows that the longest tennis rally consisted of an astounding 51,283 strokes and took over 12 hours to complete!

Those tennis players, Simone Frediani and Daniele Pecci of Italy, must have been absolute athletes to keep that rally going for so long. They were determined and even carried water on their backs and sipped the water while playing from their backpacks to stay hydrated.

They started swinging at 6:23 am and didn't finish until 7 pm. That's over 12 hours later. It's hard to imagine the monotony, endurance and stamina required for such a lengthy rally.

When they were asked how they handled using the bathroom during such a long rally, Simone revealed they wore diapers under their shorts, so they didn't have to stop.

Eventually though, even those elite athletes grew too fatigued and ran out of water, so the rally had to end. But still, over 12 hours of tennis is absolutely amazing!

Getting to the new sport of pickleball, the rally record for pickleball is along those lines. The Guinness World Record for the longest pickleball rally was set by twin brothers Angelo A. Rossetti and Ettore Rossetti, two Italian Americans from Rocky Hill, Connecticut.

Their rally on the much smaller court lasted an unbelievable 6 hours and 11 minutes and even though the time is less than the tennis rally, their pickleball rally totaled 16,046 shots! Hats off to them for their endurance, skill and determination required to rally that long in a pickleball match?

They didn't do it just for the record. Angelo and Ettore took on this grueling challenge to raise awareness for the important cause of preventing the deaths of children under 5 from treatable medical issues. What an incredible way to bring attention to such an important cause.

*The Rossetti brothers.*

**Is rugby tougher than NFL football?** Clint Eastwood told an absolutely riveting story about his uncle who played rugby with ferocity and grit, and his dad who battled on the gridiron as a tough football player, and they would engage in the most intense debates about which sport demanded the most physicality and toughness.

After many discussions and comparisons of the bone-crushing hits that each endured, everybody eventually agreed without a doubt that rugby took the crown as the roughest game around.

Clint's perspective of rugby is that it's an absolutely amazing team sport that requires total commitment and dedication from each and every player on the pitch. In order to find success, every single person on the team must give their absolute all on every single down and play with complete constructive collaboration as a cohesive unit. There is no room for slacking off or taking players off, you have to leave it all on the field if you want to win.

While each sport is unique, rugby rules provide a substituted player cannot return to the field again while NFL football allows substitutions at any time. NFL football has 11 players on a team and rugby has 15 on each team.

One major difference is that tackling techniques are different. Rugby doesn't allow high tackling and players have to wrap their arms around the lower portion of the body to bring a player to the ground. In NFL football there are many ways to tackle including shoulder tackles done at high running speeds resulting in hard collision.

NFL football players wear a lot of protective gear to avoid injuries from high running speed impacts which sometimes leads to joint sprains and fractures. Rugby players don't wear a lot of protective gear which increases the likelihood of concussions and musculoskeletal injuries.

As to which one is tougher, most feel the debate will go on and on infinitely.

## Stopping tennis balls from leaving the court.

The dark clouds of tragedy loomed over Blackfriars abbey. King James I, King of the Scots and the grandson of Robert the Bruce had sensed the growing threat to his rule, and sought refuge within the abbey's somber walls. But even there, surrounded by prayer and contemplation, he could not escape his fate.

The King enjoyed the sport of tennis, if only to distract him from his troubles for a brief moment. He played regularly at the tennis court at Blackfriars abbey. However, the tennis balls they would play with would roll off the court into a passageway which was frustrating, of course.

Frustrated and unsure of how to fix it, he chose a quick-fix solution that had fatal ramifications. His quick solution was to have the passageway blocked, caring little for what consequences his actions may bring. Workman following his orders blocked the passageway.

Later, one evening at midnight, the King sensed trouble. Assassins carrying torches approached the abbey. It turned out that they learned where he was hiding from one of his confidants who betrayed him and opened the doors for their entry.

At their lead was the traitor a Scott named Graham, who sought to end the King's rule.

King James told his loved ones to hide, though he knew it would not save them. In desperation, he tried to break the windows, but the leaded glass held fast. With a heavy heart, the King concealed himself in the only place remaining - the blocked passageway which where the tennis balls used to escape the court.

Now, it was no escape. When at last he emerged, it was into the arms of death. Though he fought with all his strength, surrounded by enemies, James' end had come. He took his final breaths knowing his kingdom would fall to chaos, and his loved ones would live on in grief and fear. [42]

So perished the doomed King, another victim of the conspiracies and betrayals that had long plagued his line. An elegy written anonymously,

Poor King James, so tragic was his fate,

By tennis balls his life did terminate.

At Blackfriars he'd play without a care,

But over the passage his balls would roll down there.

To stop their escape, the passage he blocked,

Little knowing his life would soon get docked.

For one dark night, as sleep his eyes did seize,

In came attackers, out for blood and fees.

Roused from his bed, the king knew he must flee,

But where to go to evade this tragedy?

The passage's exit offered hope of escape,

Alas the it was blocked, his doom to shape.

Caught in the tunnel like a rat in a trap,

The assassins' blades did end his royal nap.

All for some balls while playing his sport,

Now the Scot's king met his grim reap what you sow retort.

King James, King of the Scots

**You want fries with that?** Before the great Usain Bolt shocked the world by setting the unfathomable world record at that time in the 100-meter dash at the 2008 Beijing Olympics, he was fueling up on some classic McDonald's Chicken McNuggets!

During his entire stay in China for the Olympics, the rough estimated total number of Chicken McNuggets this man consumed is astonishing - he estimates he ate around 1,000 McNuggets over the entire 10 days of the greatest sporting event happening on earth!

Bolt wrote in his autobiography "The Fastest Man Alive" that "I didn't eat anything else except Chicken McNuggets in China. They didn't affect my stomach."

Usain ate them at every single meal to avoid any potential stomach issues and drank water.

In his later book "Faster than Lightning" Bolt joked "Man, I should have gotten a gold medal for all that chowing down.

Usain Bolt's famous Victory pose is so iconic! He first busted out the legendary "To Di World" pose at the 2008 Beijing Olympics and it immediately took the world by storm.

They call it the "Bolting" pose because he does it every single time after winning a race on the track. That pose is Bolt's way of dedicating his success to his millions of loyal fans who have cheered, encouraged, and supported him to victory.

You'll never believe this - at the 2008 Beijing Olympics where Bolt set the new 100m world record of 9.9 seconds, his shoelace was actually untied the entire time he was running! Can you imagine?

And get this - studies from the University of Oslo said if his shoelace hadn't slowed him down even a tiny bit while celebrating before the finish line, he could have run it in a mind-blowing 9.0 seconds!

His first love was actually cricket! He played as a fast bowler, and it was his cricket coach who noticed his incredible speed and recommended he try track instead.

Bolt was stoked to switch to athletics because he loved sports so much. He was a huge fan of legendary fast bowlers like

Waqar Younis back in the day and even idolized cricketers Chris Gayle, Sachin Tendulkar, and Matthew Hayden.

Get a load of this - Bolt has openly said he wants to play for Manchester United when he retires from running! Can you believe it? In 2012 he said if Sir Alex Ferguson called him up and asked him to try out, he'd be there.

He has nicknames "Bolt from the Blue" and "Lightning Bolt" - how fitting for the fastest man who ever lived!

Can you believe Bolt even owns his own restaurant and clothing line now? His restaurant is called "Tracks and Records" in Jamaica. His clothing brand, "Bolt Collection" has those iconic signature polo shirts with his victory pose on them. He put in the hard work and earned a great life after retiring!

You might wonder what happens if Usain Bolt ever misses a bus. The answer is his waits for it at the next stop.

Usain Bolt

**Oh, the irony!** Listen to your body, or else you may end up like the great Jim Fixx - the man who popularized running and believed it to be the cure for all ailments.

Jim began his journey to fitness later in life than most, carrying a hefty 214 pounds on his frame and smoking two full packs of cigarettes daily. What a way to live! It's no wonder the poor man's heart was in such a state.

But Jim had an idea - he would take up running and cast off his unhealthy habits.

What a noble effort! Through sweat and determination, he lost a sizable 60 pounds and kicked his nasty smoking habit to the curb. Newly svelte and smoke-free, Jim felt reborn! He just had to share his secrets to success with the masses. And thus, his bestselling book "The Complete Book of Running" was born. What wisdom it contained!

Alas, it was not meant to be. While out for a jog in 1984, at the still relatively young age of 52, Jim's enlarged heart had finally had enough. It seems those decades of abuse had taken their toll after all.

The autopsy revealed blockages as high as 95%! How ironic that the very activity Jim championed as the cure for heart disease was involved in his own untimely demise. Did he wrongly to balance healthy and unhealthy activities?

As it turns out, Jim may have had more stacked against him than just bad habits. His family history revealed a strong genetic predisposition, with his own father succumbing to heart attacks in his 30s and 40s.

If only Jim had heeded his body's warnings and listened to the cautious doctors. But who can blame a man for wanting to spread the gospel of health and wellness?

We can only hope that through Jim's tragic story, others may learn - listen to your body above all else. After all, irony has a way of finding us in the end.

**All hockey players are bilingual**. The night outside Madison Square Garden was alive with energy. There were tales of intense battles waging within those very walls and many are eager to witness the spectacle. Taking a seat, one realizes this was no ordinary fight.

The crowd roared with a ferocity to match the combatants below. These were no mere brawlers trading blows - they glided across the ice with lightning speed, twirling and spinning in a deadly dance. Sticks slashed through the air, connecting with puck in a flurry of precision. It was a well-choreographed assault played out at a breakneck pace. This was no fight - this was a hockey game, and what a game it was!

According to Gordie Howe, hockey players speak two languages - “English and profanity.”

Gordie Howe aka "Mr. Hockey" and considered to one of the greatest and most complete players to ever play the game. The NY Rangers invited him to try out camp when he was 15 years old. He played in the National Hockey League All Star Game 23 times which is the most times of any player.

Gordie Howe

**Surfing is about inner satisfaction**. The ocean swells rose that fateful Tahitian morning, a harbinger of challenges to come. Laird Hamilton gazed out at the Teahupo'o break, its turbulent waters brimming with danger and opportunity. This was a wave like no other, a monster that had swallowed men whole. But Laird was no ordinary man. He was a big wave legend, possessed of a courage and skill.

As the sun rose over that distant isle, Laird's supporter Darrick prepared their vessel. All eyes were on the surf master, waiting to see if he would attempt to tame the beast. With a nod to Darrick, the moment was set. Laird was towed into the maw of the wave, descending into its roiling depths. The vortex swallowed him whole, and all watched with bated breath. Would this be the day the wave claimed another victim?

But then, emerging from the tunnel, Laird was seen! Carving perfectly upon the wave's shoulder, his form was poetry in motion. Gasps of awe rose from all who witnessed this spectacle. Laird had stared down the monster and survived, his mastery complete. The photographs would cement his legend for all time. None could ride waves like Laird Hamilton, a man who defied death's grasp again and again in pursuit of inner satisfaction.

Back on shore, Laird would reflect on the day's triumph. "At the end, it is not what others say that matters most. True satisfaction comes from within.  Laird lived only to challenge the impossible and please his soul. In those moments atop giant mountains of water, all the world fell away but the ride. This was Laird's domain, and his alone.

**How many tennis balls are used at Wimbledon?** Believe it or not, about 54,000 balls are used in the tournament. The balls are looked at closely during play to make sure there is no damage and replaced every seven to nine games to ensure the players are using balls in top condition.

They sell the balls afterwards in a can of three for about 2-3 pounds to the public. Not a bad price!

**Marathon.** I decided to run the NYC Marathon. After the race started, I found myself in last place, and it was embarrassing.

This guy in front of me was second to last and taunting me saying, “Hey pal, how’s it feel to be last?”

I said, “You really want to know?”

Then I dropped out of the race.

**Alternative to the Indy 500**. While Indy cars are hitting speeds of over 200 mph, there is another highly unique race that was conceptualized in a pub.

As the legend goes, in 1973 the great Formula One driver Jackie "The Flying Scot" Stewart dominated the season, winning three world championships.

Meanwhile, across the English Channel, a ragtag group of would-be racers in West Sussex were drowning their dreams of motorsport glory in pints of ale at the local pub. As the beers flowed, they started fantasizing about how to make racing more accessible for the average bloke. That's when someone had a truly brilliant idea - lawnmower racing!

While that seems hilarious at first as you can imagine a bunch of lads zooming around a track on riding mowers, this eccentric idea caught on! Soon the British Lawn Mower Racing Association (BLRA) was formed. They have an entire championship series running from May to October, with 30 races held at rural events like the Cranleigh Show in Surrey. There spectators can also see other classic British pastimes like ferret racing. The blades are taken off the mowers for safety reasons.

The BLRA remains committed to their grassroots roots (pun intended), donating all profits to charity and encouraging spectators to pack a picnic.

One special event is the BLMRA 12-hour endurance race. It's been held near a place called Wisborough Green in England since 1978. The very professional driver Sir Stirling Moss, Derek Bell, and Tony Hazlewood won the first race. Tony was actually the designer and builder of the car they used, which was called the Westwood Lawnbug. Actor Oliver Reed took part in it one time.

It attracts racers from all over the place. Other British racing clubs come out for it as well as folks from France, Belgium, Germany, Luxembourg, Finland, and the US. A conversation over a pint of ale in a pub creating a sport has spread throughout the world! Keep that in mind that the next time you're having a beer after a game the conversation turns to new sports.

In 2018, the winner actually was someone from overseas for the first time in the whole history of the event.

As for records, the farthest distance driven over the 12-hour period is 354 miles. Think of the amount of grass that would be cut!

So, while Indy cars are living fast and furious, over the pond they're keeping it real -- and hilarious -- on their trusty lawnmowers. Talk about mowing down the competition!

Lawnmower racing.

**Bowling**. Bowling has been around for a very long time. Archeologists have found evidence that suggests the sport may date back as far as 3200 BC. In some ancient Egyptian tombs, they discovered objects that resembled the pins we use for bowling today. There were also hieroglyphics on the walls of these tombs that seemed to depict people participating in an activity that looked a lot like bowling.

Fast forward to the 1700s. Getting three strikes in a row, what we now call a "turkey", has an interesting origin for its name. In the late 1700s and 1800s, bowling tournaments were a very popular pastime in both Europe and America. The winners of these tournaments would often receive baskets filled with food as their prize.

But striking wasn't as easy back then as it is with our modern bowling alleys that have smooth, perfectly level lanes. The balls used were also not as well-balanced as the ones we have now. So, during one of these early tournaments, the players started to realize that anyone who was able to bowl three strikes in a row had a really good chance of winning the food basket prize, which usually contained a turkey.

And so, the achievement of three consecutive strikes became known as a "turkey".

Recreational bowlers may not be familiar with terms for other impressive strike streaks.

- Four strikes in a row is called a "hambone".
- Five strikes with no spares is known as a "brat".
- Six strikes in a row is dubbed a "wild turkey" or a "six pack".
- Seven strikes earns the label "turkey-ham dinner".
- An amazing eight strikes with no spares between is an "octopus".
- Nine strikes is the coveted "golden turkey".
- And of course, rolling twelve perfect strikes for an entire game is considered a "dinosaur".

While no one actually ate dinosaurs for their perfect game, the term was used because such an accomplishment is about as rare as a living dinosaur!

**I want that guy… give me a paper napkin!** The director of the Barcelona football team really wanted this young new kid named Lionel Messi after seeing him during the trial to make the Barcelona team.

Messi's family had connections through relatives in Catalonia that got him the opportunity for a tryout in September 2000. Well, the kid must have really impressed because the director since the director simply said, "I want that guy!"

Unfortunately, he didn't have any paper contracts on him at the time. Can you believe it, he wrote Messi's very first contract on a paper napkin! Talk about informal.

But it worked out because Messi went on to make his debut for Barcelona against their rivals Espanyol when he was only 17 years old. That made Messi the third youngest player ever to start for Barcelona. However, Messi went beyond that when he also became the absolute youngest player in the club's history to score a goal.

On Messi's 18th birthday, he signed his first real contract as a senior team player. And this one was on actual paper, I'm sure.

The buy-out clause was set at a hefty €150 million euros and the contract was extended until 2010. So, Barcelona was definitely committing to Messi as an important part of their future plans.

Little did they know at the time just how huge of a star he would become!

Lionel Messi

**Ronaldo is named after Ronald Reagan**. Like Lionel Messi, Cristiano Ronaldo did not come from money. Born in Sao Pedro parish of Funchal, his father was a gardener and had alcohol problems and died of liver failure in 2005. His mother was a cook. Ronaldo's childhood was difficult.

Rinaldo eventually became the first soccer player billionaire. This happened in 2020 when he surpassed over $1 billion in earnings. What an incredible achievement, considering where he began in life.

Few know that he was named after Ronald Reagan. He said his parents named him after Ronald Reagan because his parents liked that name and it sounded strong.

Interestingly, he said his father was already a big fan of Reagan way before he became the President of the United States, as Reagan was his favorite actor.

**No confidence**. If self-depreciation was a sport. I'd probably be pretty rubbish at that too. And, if having low confidence and low self-esteem was an Olympic sport. I would probably get bronze.

**Young Tiger.** The young Tiger Woods had incredible golf accomplishments. So much has been written and discussed about Tiger that few remember his beginnings as a true prodigy.

He made his national TV debut before age three -- that's just unheard of! But his most amazing early feat had to be scoring his first ever hole-in-one at only six years old.

Now that's where things get interesting because even Tiger seemed to misremember how old he was. When asked during a golf clinic, he told everyone it was at eight years old. But we've done the math and checked the records - it definitely happened on May 12th, 1982, when he was 6 as a first grader, that's just insane.

Tiger and his father, Earl Woods in later years.

**Sports Quiz Question 6.** In which Olympic sport might you hear the term "Press out"?

A. Basketball

B. Gymnastics - horizontal bar.

C. Weightlifting.

D. Archery.

*Answer on p. 200*

**Tigerfish tournament.** [43] Tigerfish are the jungle's apex predator. Deep in the waterways of Africa lurks a monster - a fish so fearsome it has earned the moniker "Tiger of the Waters."

I speak of course of the Tigerfish, a savage beast that strikes terror into the hearts of all who dwell near its domain. With razor-edged fangs and muscles of coiled steel, this killer cuts through schools of prey with brutal efficiency. Stories are told of Tigerfish leaping from the rivers to drag squawking avians into a watery grave, its vice-like jaws crushing bone.

*Tigerfish*

Once a year, the hardiest of anglers gather for a trial of skills and nerves against this aquatic tyrant. Fishermen from every corner of the globe converge on Lake Kariba, where the largest of the Tigerfish, Hydrocynus Goliath, grows to truly monstrous size.

For three days they battle their catches, competing not only against the ferocity of the Tigerfish, but against each other with boats having to stay at least 100 meters apart.

Only those with nerves of steel and a mastery of line and lure can emerge victorious from this contest of hunter and hunted.

When at last the sun sinks on the final day and the lines are reeled in, the victor will be crowned before returning to await another year's challenge against the King of Kariba's deadly domain.

The tournament was started in 1962 is now considered to be the largest single-species four-man Fresh Water Fishing tournament in the world. [44]

**Ever catch a fish with a snake?** Talk about unusual baits and weird fishing using a slithering snake!

Now I know what you're thinking - using a live snake for bait is just plain nuts. But I came across this video that will make you do a double take! Check this crazy video out on YouTube referenced in the endnotes. [45]

Poor thing is dangling off the line, looking mighty confused. But our fisherman has a plan - he lowers Snakezilla into the water and waits.

It doesn't take long before an unsuspecting fish goes in for a bite. But it gets more than it bargained for! That snake latches on with its teeth and starts constricting a bit like its life depends on it. Which, you know, it kind of does at this point.

You never know what people will use to catch their dinner. There are some really aggressive and hungry snakes out there! Live frogs, mice, even other fish - if it moves, put it on your hook and see what results.

It doesn't take long before an unsuspecting fish goes in for a bite. But it gets more than it bargained for! That snake latches on with its teeth and starts constricting like its life depends on it. Which, you know, it kind of does at this point.

**Mexican Professional Wrestling**. Lucha libre, or as we gringos like to call it, Mexican Wrasslin'! Part sport, part soap opera on the mat, lucha libre is a wild blend of acrobatic moves and more drama than your average telenovela.

The competitors, or luchadores, are known for their outlandish masks that would put any WWE superstar to shame. But unlike those guys up north, these masked men keep their identities secret! That's until they're thrown out of the ring in a high-flyin' match, at which point the loser has to reveal his face like a criminal snatching off a ski mask.

And it doesn't stop there, oh no! If a luchador really disgraces himself, he might find his precious locks shaved clean off like a barbershop floor. Talk about ignominy! But it sure is fun to watch.

With the crowd fueled by tequila and passion for lucha libre, the atmosphere is more of a fiesta than a fight. The spectators get so riled up they start chucking coins into the ring whenever their favorite wrestler pins an opponent. It's like it's raining pesos!

The victorious luchador then collects up the moolah, no doubt to spend on more fabulous masks and outrageous costumes. So, grab a cerveza and some small change, my friends - it's time for the greatest soap opera south of the border: Lucha Libre!

Competitor in Lucha Libre

**Most viewed sports events in the world.** The most viewed sporting events in the world never cease to amaze with their jaw-dropping viewership numbers. Some of these top 10 sports events might surprise you with just how many eyeballs they attract, and some may not.

- Kicking things off at number one is the event of events -- the FIFA World Cup of Soccer. With a staggering 5 billion viewers, you better believe the entire globe comes to a screeching halt every four years to watch international soccer supremacy be decided.

  The competition and drama is simply unmatched. The next World cup returns to North America for the 2026 World Cup hosted by Canada, Mexico and the United States.

- In at number two is the grueling Tour de France cycling race with an incredible 3 billion viewers glued to their screens. I am constantly in awe of the sheer physical and mental strength these athletes display as they pedal hundreds of miles over multiple stages. The 2024 Tour de France promises to be just as epic.

- Coming in third is the Cricket World Cup attracting a massive 2 billion viewers. As I'm more of a baseball fan, I have to admit my surprise at seeing cricket on this list! But with 10 teams competing in it over six exhilarating weeks, it's no wonder the Cricket World Cup is such a global phenomenon. It truly is a sporting extravaganza!

- In the number four spot is the FIFA Women's World Cup exploding in popularity with a viewership of 2 billion. The 2023 tournament saw numbers nearly double from 2019, which is absolutely incredible. In fact, the China vs. England match alone drew an astounding 53 million viewers in China, setting a new record!

With women's sports on the rise, I can't wait to see what new heights the excitement reaches at the next Women's World Cup in 2027.

- And of course, coming in at number five are the awe-inspiring Summer Olympic Games attracting a colossal 2 billion viewers every two years. From track and field to swimming to gymnastics and more, there is truly no greater global sports festival that stirs our competitive spirits and celebrates human achievement like the Summer Games. If you are a fan of Olympic games, the next Summer Games for 2024 will be held in the magnificent city of Paris!

- The Winter Olympics deserve just as much praise, clocking in at number six with another 2 billion viewers tuning in to see snow and ice sports contested at the highest level.

Even though winter sports may not have the same mainstream appeal as their summer counterparts, the Winter Games continue to enthrall audiences around the world every four years. The next 2026 Winter Olympics take place in the gorgeous settings of Milano Cortina.

- At number seven is the UEFA Champions League Final with a whopping 450 million viewers for the 2023 match alone. As the most prestigious club competition in soccer, it's easy to understand why the Champions League Final is such a momentous event. The 2024 Final in London promises more nail-biting action between European giants.

- In the eighth spot is the granddaddy of them all in the US -- the Super Bowl! With a record-shattering 115 million viewers in 2023, it's no secret why Super Bowl Sunday has become our unofficial national holiday.

  From the game itself to the commercials and halftime show, the Super Bowl is the perfect mix of entertainment and tradition. The next Super Bowl LVII is taking place in the bright lights of Las Vegas!

- Ninth on the list is the illustrious Wimbledon tennis championships drawing in 25 million viewers each year to watch the world's best battle on grass courts. As the most famous tennis tournament on the planet, it's also the most attended - over 532,000 fans soaked up the on-court magic live in 2023 alone. The 2024 edition will of course be at Wimbledon July 1 -- 14$^{th.}$!

- And finally, rounding things out with 17 million viewers is the NBA Finals! After an epic 82-game regular season and grueling playoff battles, only two teams are left standing to decide basketball supremacy.

With incredible athletes, celebrities, and energy, it's no wonder the NBA Finals captivate sports fans worldwide. Next NBA Finals: June 2024.

**What an incredible hockey story of perseverance and triumph** over adversity! David Ayres, a true hockey hero, showed the world that with determination and heart, anything is possible.

Can you believe it? At the time, David was 42 years old and driving the Zamboni machine (clears the ice). Just a few years before, he received a life-saving kidney transplant. Suddenly, he was thrust into the spotlight and called upon to lead Carolina to victory in an NHL game! It's almost unbelievable, but I assure you every word is true.

Ayres was just doing his job, keeping the ice pristine for practices as the on-call emergency backup goalie. Little did he know that fate had bigger plans for him that night. When both Hurricanes goalies went down with injuries, the coaches came calling for Ayres. Though shocked, he sprang into action without hesitation. Still half dressed, he raced to the arena, phone blowing up the whole way.

Stepping between the pipes, you just knew this was his moment. Adrenaline pumping, heart racing, he was ready to give it his all for Carolina. And give it his all he did!

Though he let in a couple early ones as he settled in, he then stood on his head making save after incredible save. The crowd, once cheering against him, was now fully behind this true underdog story.

When the final buzzer sounded and the Hurricanes emerged victorious, the celebration was on. Ayres had etched his name in the record books that night, becoming the oldest goalie ever to win his NHL debut. But more than that, he inspired millions with his perseverance and courage in the face of adversity. He is living proof that dreams can come true against all odds if you never give up the fight. A true hero among men and forever a legend in Carolina!

**Gentleman Bobby Pearce.** It was a beautiful summer day at the 1928 Olympics in Amsterdam. The rowing events were underway on the Stoten Canal. Australian rower Bobby Pearce was focused as he powered through the quarterfinal race. Victory at the Olympics had long been his dream.

Suddenly, Pearce heard cries from the nearby bank. He turned and was met with an unexpected sight - a mother duck followed by a line of little ducklings waddling right into the path of the oncoming boats. Pearce's heart swelled with compassion. He couldn't bear to continue on and risk harming the precious creatures.

Slowing his boat, Pearce called out "Slow down boys, let the ducks pass safely!". His opponent Sauurin saw his chance and surged ahead, taking a substantial lead. But Pearce didn't care about winning at that moment - all that mattered was protecting the duck family. Once the last duckling had crossed, he called out "You're clear, resume the race!".

Though far behind, Pearce dug deep and poured on speed, pulling fiercely at the oars. He had an extra motivation now -

to prove that compassion need not come at the cost of victory. Meter by meter he gained on Sauurin. With thunderous cheers and applause ringing out, Pearce crossed the finish line a full 30 seconds ahead, having staged a remarkable comeback.

His act of kindness towards the ducks would only add to his legend. Pearce went on to win the finals and retain his title as world champion for an incredible 12 years. Though nearly a century has passed, the story of Bobby Pearce and the ducks lives on as a heartwarming reminder that even in our fiercest competitions, there is always room for mercy, courage and goodwill towards others.

**Bobby Jones and St. Andrews.** Before he founded the Augusta National Golf Club, the legendary Bobby Jones first stepped foot upon the hallowed grounds of the Old Course at St Andrews in 1921, arriving as a young but talented amateur to compete in that year's Open Championship.

During the third round, Jones found himself in a spot of bother after his approach shot landed in a treacherous bunker on the par-four 11th hole.

After flailing away four times in the sand yet unable to escape, the pressure and frustration got the better of the man, and he angrily stormed off to continue his round.

However, in a show of sportsmanship and humility, Jones chose not to submit his scorecard, eliminating himself from contention in an act of self-imposed disqualification.

Undaunted, Jones returned to St Andrews six years later a wiser and more experienced player. What transpired was nothing short of legendary, as the American amateur proceeded to dominate the field from start to finish.

Posting a record-setting total of 285 shots over four days, a whopping seven-under-par at the time, Jones cruised to victory by a cavernous six shot margin.

It was a masterful performance that announced to the world this was no ordinary player. Jones had fallen in love with the Old Course, and it seemed the feeling was mutual.

Four years later in 1930, Bobby Jones was back at St Andrews competing in the British Amateur Championship. In a storybook ending, Jones emerged victorious after defeating Roger Wethered 7 and 6 in the final match.

For the remainder of his life, Jones held a deep admiration for the Old Course, often remarking that if given one match to define his career, it would be played on its hallowed links.

In a moving tribute to the man's impact, the town of St Andrews bestowed upon Jones one of golf's highest honors in 1958 -- being awarded the key to the city, making him only the second American ever to receive the accolade.

With humility and grace, Jones acknowledged this was due to his experiences and success on the Old Course alone, which enriched his life immensely.

Bobby Jones' legend was forever intertwined with St Andrews, the home of golf, where a young man once walked and achieved sporting immortality.

Bobby Jones

**Sports Quiz Question 7**. What country in the world has the longest life expectancy and whose national sport is soccer? Hine: they also favor motor racing, yachting, and tennis.

A. Portugal

B. Spain

C. Japan

D. Monaco

E. South Korea

F. None of the above.

*Answer on p. 200*

**Going out in style**. It was a bittersweet day on October 1st, 1977, as soccer legend Pele played his final match. The friendly exhibition between his former clubs, New York Cosmos and Santos, held much more significance than a typical friendly.

Though Pele originally hailed from Brazil, he had found a home across the ocean in America after being persuaded by the Secretary of Foreign Affairs to bring his talents stateside and grow the beautiful game in the United States. He joined the Cosmos in 1975 and immediately became a superstar.

By the time of his retirement, Pele was viewed by many as nearly divine for his accomplishments on the pitch. Even the great Muhammad Ali, one of the most iconic athletes of all time, made the trip to witness Pele's swan song.

The match began with Pele wearing the green and white of Santos, and he delighted fans with a vintage goal for his boyhood club. At halftime, he emotionally switched kits to don the blue of the Cosmos, capping his time in America.

As the final whistle blew, ending Pele's incomparable career, tears flowed freely from all in attendance. His fellow players wept as they embraced their legend of a teammate, while supporters sobbed at the realization, they'd never again see Pele perform his magic on the field.

The next day, newspapers reported the heavy rain that fell from the sky during the second half. "Even the sky was crying" one headline poetically declared. Truly, it was impossible for anyone present, or anyone who loved the beautiful game of soccer, not to feel deep sorrow at having to say goodbye to the greatest of all time. Pele's farewell match was a heartwarming yet heartbreaking celebration of a player who transcended sports.

Edson Arantes do Nascimento (Pele)

**Let's share**. The crowd roared as the pole vault competition at the 1938 Berlin Olympics was coming to a dramatic close. The gold medal was already secured by American star Earle Meadows, who soared to an incredible height of 4.5 meters. But who would claim silver and bronze?

Another American, Bill Sefton, and two friends from Japan, Shuhei Nishida and Sueo Oe, were the last three competitors remaining. Sefton took his final jump but couldn't clear the bar, ending his medal hopes. Now it was down to Nishida and Oe, the Japanese duo, to battle it out.

Nishida and Oe had trained together for years, pushing each other to greater heights. But this was more than just a competition - this was a test of their friendship. Both Nishida and Oe sailed over the 4. 5-meter bar, tying for second place. A tiebreaker jump was proposed to decide silver versus bronze.

To the crowd's surprise, Nishida and Oe refused to participate in the tiebreaker. They were friends first, competitors second. They wanted to share the honor of medaling for their country. However, the officials denied their request, saying medals had to be awarded.

After long discussion, the Japanese team decided. Given that Nishida cleared the height on his first try while Oe needed two attempts, Nishida was awarded silver. Oe received bronze. But the friends were not satisfied with this resolution.

When they returned home to Japan, in a moving display of friendship, Nishida and Oe cut their medals in half and fused them together. Now, each athlete possessed a medal that was half silver, half bronze - a symbol of their bond that transcended sport. It was a triumph not just of athleticism, but of humanity.

**Too much golf**. A wife was terribly upset because her husband, Joe, neglected her for years, played too much golf, and always came home late. So, she decided to take a stand and leave a note,

*"Joe, I've had enough of your neglect. You play golf too much. I am leaving you. Don't bother looking for me, I'm gone."*

Suddenly, she heard him coming in, so she scurried and hid under the bed curious to see his reaction.

Joe enters their home. She hears him in the kitchen and then his steps into their bedroom where she's hiding. She sees him walk towards the dresser and pick up the note.

Joe writes something on the note before picking up the phone and then makes a call.

"Hi baby! She's gone at last! I'll be over to see you darling and put on that lace I like. I'm almost out the door and will be on your doorstep right away!"

He hangs up the phone, takes his keys, and leaves.

She hears him drive off and in a total rage comes out and snatches the note from the dresser and reads what he wrote,

*"I can see your feet. We're out of milk. Be back in ten minutes."*

**Three Unworldly Golf Courses.** Are you a long hitter seeking an epic challenge? Then look no further than the courses that push the very limits of the game.

The first is located high in the Himalayas of China - the Dragon Snow Mountain Golf Club in Lijiang. Situated at over 10,000 feet, its thin air allows golf drives to soar farther than ever imagined.

Yet its beauty is matched only by its unforgiving terrain. Towering peaks encircle each hole, their jagged silhouettes a stark reminder of the heights one must conquer.

Here, the shortest par 3 stretches a staggering 236 yards and the longest hole a mind-bending 711!

Oxygen is needed merely to walk the course, let alone face its trials.

Its designers, Robin Nelson and Neil Haworth, crafted a masterwork befitting the mighty mountains.

The second course is a cliff top course in the Southern Pacific Ocean. The windswept cliffs of Cape Kidnappers call out to any soul yearning for natural splendor and solitude. Stretching endlessly into the vast sea, its grassy headlands and wooded gullies now ring with the songs of native species (Kiwi birds and other rare birds) restored to abundance.

Here man and beast live not at odds but in harmony. While golfers seek challenge on windswept fairways, all reap reward of conservation's fruits. The picture below of the $12^{th}$ through the 16th holes is worth a thousand words.

Cape Kidnappers GC, Hawkes Bay, New Zealand

The third course lies not in the heights but across the vast emptiness of Australia's interior. Stretching over 1,365 kilometers along the Eyre Highway, the Nullarbor Links is truly golf's final frontier.

Where others see only desert, founders Alf Caputo and Bob Bongiorno envisioned a course spanning two states and all the nothingness in between. Professional Robert Stock then drew the impossible - incorporating roadhouses and remote stations into 18 holes.

Here, the average distance between holes is a mind-boggling 66 km! The largest gap of nearly 200 km is a journey unto itself.

One hole sits amidst a sheep station with views of the shearing shed and roaming flocks. But dangers also await off the fairways - crows, emus, snakes, eagles and the ever-present threat of wombat holes lurk in the brush.

And as if the course itself did not provide enough challenge, temperatures often exceed 50 degrees Celsius (122 degrees F)!

So, for those seeking not just a game but an epic quest, these two courses beckon. Where ordinary golf dares do not venture, they push the boundaries of possibility.

For the long hitter seeking to conquer not just the course but the natural world itself, these are challenges for the ages.

Nullarbor Links, Hole 6, Border Village, South Australia

**Jesse Owens.** Most everyone knows the amazing story of Jesse Owens. During the infamous 1936 Berlin Olympic Games, the evil Nazis ridiculed the United States for relying on "non-human Black auxiliaries. But they didn't know what was coming!

The American Black athlete Jesse Owens was about to put on the most incredible athletic display the world had ever seen. When he won an unprecedented FOUR gold medals and beat a German athlete in the long jump with Hitler watching in person, it was absolutely epic! Four years after Owens' passing, as a tribute to his greatness, a street in Berlin was renamed in his honor.

Can you believe what Jesse Owens did just one year before the Berlin Olympics? It was an ordinary spring afternoon in 1935 when Owens literally rewrote the history books by smashing THREE world records and tying another, all within just 45 minutes! That's right - he dominated the competition so thoroughly that day that THREE world records fell to him in under an hour. After a performance like that, you just knew 1936 was going to be his year!

And did he ever deliver the next summer in Berlin! With the evil Nazis and their propaganda machine in full force, infusing the entire city and stadium with their hateful ideology, Owens was ready to show the world what a true champion looks like. As the Nazi anthem played and those terrifying red and black swastikas flew overhead, with Hitler himself watching from the stands, Owens went to work.

The African American grandson of slaves achieved his incredible victories despite the heavy Nazi aura hanging over the entire event. Owens singlehandedly destroyed the Nazi's twisted idea of Aryan supremacy, winning gold after gold. The look on Hitler's face must have been priceless as Owens dominated one event after another. It was the ultimate moment of embarrassment for the Nazis, who had complained that the "non-humans" like Owens shouldn't even be allowed to compete. But compete he did, and in the process cemented his place as one of the greatest athletes of all time!

Owens' performance in Berlin was nothing short of legendary. He captured an unprecedented at the time four gold medals at a single Olympics, winning the 100m, long jump, 200m, and anchoring the 4x100m relay team to victory. A feat that wouldn't be matched for almost 50 years until Carl Lewis equaled it at the 1984 Los Angeles Games!

On top of that, did you know Owens raced to gold wearing German-made track shoes crafted by the founder of Adidas himself? That's right, even the German shoemaker Adi Dassler recognized Owens' greatness and helped launch his company by getting Owens to wear the handmade leather spikes. A decade later, Adidas was born, in part thanks to Jesse Owens' inspirational performance. The story of Jesse Owens is one of perseverance, courage and determination in the face of unbelievable adversity.

Did you know that at just 5 years old, Owens' parents had to perform emergency surgery on him using just a kitchen knife to remove a golf ball sized growth from his chest? And he survived! His mother removed it while little Jesse was biting down on a leather strap.

Despite facing racism and being barred from the campus dorms at Ohio State because of his skin color, Owens nevertheless broke records and became a champion.

At the Big Ten Championships in 1935, Jesse was on fire Not only did he tie a world record in the 100-yard dash, but get this - just 15 minutes later he completely destroyed the long jump world record by almost six inches! Are you kidding me?! That's insane.

But he wasn't done yet. Within the next half hour, this incredible athlete also set two more world records in the 220-yard dash and the 220-yard low hurdles. All of this he did with a severely injured tailbone! Can you imagine being in such pain but still performing at such a high level? He must have just been in the zone and powering through the pain. What an amazing display of athleticism. To set three world records and tie another all within 45 minutes is absolutely unheard of. Talk about being in the zone and being completely locked in on competition day.

Jesse Owens was a true champion and showed what an incredible athlete he was that day in Ann Arbor. What a phenomenal performance to remember forever. You have to just tip your cap to such an amazing display of speed, strength, and determination.

Jesse Owens cemented his place in history with his legendary performance at the 1936 Berlin Olympics, where he singlehandedly destroyed Hitler's twisted vision of Aryan supremacy. He inspired generations and continues to be remembered as one of the greatest and most courageous athletes of all time!

Jesse Owens

**Gentleman and ah…you too, Miss, start your engines!** Maria Teresa de Filippis accomplished the commendable title of the first woman to participate in Formula One, and what an accomplishment it was!

While her Grand Prix career was relatively short-lived at only five races total, she blazed a trail for all the amazing women drivers who have come after her.

Four of Filippis' races were held in 1958 with her last one in 1959. What courage and determination it must have taken for her to break into such a male-dominated sport then.

Maria Teresa de Filippis is legendary in motorsports history and is forever associated with her incredible Maserati 250F vehicle. They don't call the 250F one of the fastest and most beautiful racing cars ever built for nothing - this machine was a true work of art on wheels. It helped propel Filippis' friend, the great Juan Manuel Fangio, to his record-setting fifth world championship title. Talk about being in control of a race car destined for glory!

Maria Teresa de Filippis

Filippis boldly competed for the first time in 1958, a time when safety precautions at the circuits were certainly not what they are today. However, she fearlessly proved that women had just as much skill and nerve behind the wheel as any man, racing at astonishing speeds of 175 miles per hour! Despite the very real risks to life and limb, Filippis was undeterred in her quest to highlight women's talents in motorsports.

Coming from a wealthy family in Naples, Filippis' racing career began through the encouragement of her daredevil brothers. Her natural talent and bravery shone through as she took on the challenges of Formula One. Maria Teresa de Filippis' pioneering accomplishments lit the way for female drivers everywhere. She deserves to be celebrated as a true legend of the track!

Maserati 250F

**The Avid Golfer.** The groom to be is next to his bride to be at the church altar. The minister greets them and tells them to take a deep breath. As the bride exhales, she notices a set of golf clubs off to the side near the door.

“Those are your golf clubs, aren’t they?”

“Yes, they are.”

“What are they doing here?!” She asks.

“This isn’t going to take all day, is it?”

## A few intriguing NFL items.

- The legendary Terrible Towel began as a silly publicity stunt but has become an iconic symbol of Pittsburgh pride that super fans wave with ferocity at every game.

  Not only that, but devoted fans have taken their black and gold towels into the stratosphere, with one bold supporter bringing a Towel aboard the International Space Station! You can find Steeler Nation representing everywhere, even in orbit!
- When it comes to America's favorite pastime of sports betting, nearly 8 in 10 bettors place their wagers on NFL matchups, making it the most gambled on league in the US.

- While football is an exhilarating sport to play, it also leads to injury more than any other, with over 3 million football-related visits to ERs each year. Ouch!

- The venerable Green Bay Packers stand alone as the NFL's oldest team to retain their name and hometown since joining the league over a century ago in 1921. Alongside the Cards and historic Bears, the Packers are the only franchise to celebrate over 100 seasons proudly repping the same city. That small-town loyalty is simply legendary.

  Speaking of legendary, the Packers have dominated the gridiron for decades while proudly calling Green Bay, Wisconsin home. With 11 league titles and 4 Super

Bowl rings, they've won more games than any other NFL squad.

- As the 2023 season approaches, the Dallas Cowboys reign as the NFL's most valuable team after generating over $1 billion in revenue last year. That big Texas money is no surprise.

- But no achievement can top the 1972 Miami Dolphins' perfection. As the only team in NFL history to go undefeated over a full regular AND postseason, finishing 14-0 and hoisting the Lombardi, their "Perfect Season" stands alone as one of the most astonishing records in all of sports. Led by ringmaster coach Don Shula and field general QB Bob Griese with safety Jake Scott securing Super Bowl MVP honors, the '72 Dolphins were truly unstoppable.

- Just four short years after the devastation of Hurricane Katrina, the New Orleans Saints brought the city pride and joy by marching straight into Super Bowl XLIV for their first ever championship title. Behind the masterful play of QB Drew "Breesus" Brees and his 32 completions for 2 TDs, the Saints stunned the Colts 31-17. Brees' brilliance would make him the league's highest paid player in subsequent seasons. What a comeback story!

- Known affectionately as "Mr. Tom Terrific," Brady cemented his status as the undisputed GOAT with a career defined by records too numerous to list and achievements that elevated him among the pantheon of all sports legends. As he recently rode off into the sunset, the Football world bids a fond farewell to The One who took Terrific to titanic new heights.

- In a feat unmatched before or since, Washington kicker Mark "Money" Moseley struck gold in the 1982 season by becoming the sole special teams player to ever win the MVP award. How'd he do it? By breaking records with 20 field goals in 21 attempts for a mind-boggling 95% completion rate. Some kicks are more legendary than others - this one took the cake!

Mark Moseley

After several weeks of trying to work up the courage, Joe finally convinced the smokin' hot receptionist at his tennis club to let him take her out for some dinner and drinks.

Joe spared no expense wanting to score some major points, so he rented the loudest sports car he could find, dressed in the only polo shirt that still fit after last weekend's kegger, and took her to Applebee's.

However, she seemed less than impressed by his vast intellect and charm, and Joe soon realized she was way out of his pay grade. The conversation during dinner was about as lively as the country club board meeting minutes. Joe could tell she knew the only action he was used to was playing beer pong.

He excused himself to the bathroom, but on his way, he spotted tennis legend Maria Sharapova eating with some other athletes. This gave Joe an idea.

"Yo Sharapova, I know I'm interrupting your dinner, but I thought you might be kind enough to help me out with an issue I'm having with my date?" The waiter walked over but Maria shooed him away, saying "For romance issues, I'm always down to assist. What's up?"

"See that beautiful woman at my table? I've been trying to make a hit with her since the first time I saw her in the locker room. But this date is going worse than my tennis game -- I'm down two sets and serving 0-5 in the third set. Think you could swing by and pretend we're old pals? I heard she loves you and it would totally score points for me."

Maria laughed and replied, "Sure, why not? Go chill and I'll give her the eye wink and come say what's up."

Joe couldn't thank her enough and high tailed it back to his date. No sooner had he sat down than Maria yelled out a tennis scream and said, "Joe my man, is that you?!"

Joe's date looked over and exclaimed, "No way, is that Maria Sharapova?!"

Joe nodded coolly.

Maria sauntered over and said, "Joe baby, I haven't seen you at the yacht club in forever! Where you been hiding? I've missed you so much! How long has it been?!"

Joe waved her off, replying "Listen Sharapova, I told you before and I'm not gonna say it again - we're not a thing! I wish you the best but please chill, you're making me look bad in front of my date. Thanks!"

**The Ancient Sport of Pankration -- predecessor to Mixed Martial Arts.** Taking place at the ancient Greek Olympics, pankration combined boxing and wrestling into an almost no-holds-barred event. Very few techniques were actually prohibited -- competitors could not gouge eyes or bite, and attacks to the genitals were forbidden. Beyond those limitations, fighters were free to use virtually any technique to defeat their opponent.

One legendary pankration champion was a man named Arrhichion from the city of Phigalia. He first won the Olympic title in 572 BC and successfully defended it again in 568 BC. Arrhichion sought to achieve the rare feat of winning three consecutive pankration championships at the 564 BC Olympics. He advanced through the early rounds, but in the title match, age began to catch up with the veteran fighter.

In the championship bout, Arrhichion faced his toughest challenge yet. His younger opponent gained the upper hand, maneuvering behind Arrhichion and locking his legs around the champion's torso. Sinking his heels into Arrhichion's groin, the upstart then applied a chokehold. Things looked dire for the two-time defending title holder. However, Arrhichion had been in perilous situations before and still had some tricks up his sleeve.

Pretending to lose consciousness, Arrhichion fooled his opponent into loosening his grip slightly. Seeing an opening, the cagey veteran mustered his remaining strength for a Hail Mary move. With an explosive thrust, Arrhichion managed to shake off his opponent - but in the process, snapped his own ankle from the force. The excruciating pain from his broken ankle caused Arrhichion's opponent to tap out in submission.

Unfortunately for Arrhichion, as he threw off his opponent, the latter still had a chokehold locked in. The champion's neck broke during the scramble, and he collapsed dead in the ring. Since his opponent had surrendered, Arrhichion was awarded the victory posthumously - a bizarre and tragic outcome, but one that cemented his legend as the only competitor in Olympic history to win after death. He had taken the athletic ideal of "victory or death" to its literal conclusion.

Ancient artifact

**Dime Beer - not a good idea!** The Cleveland Indians were desperate to pack the stands in 1974, so they thought "Hey, how about a Dime Beer Night?" What could possibly go wrong? They'd done a nickel beer promotion in '71 with no fuss. But pairing dirt cheap booze with their bitter rivals, the Texas Rangers, the promotion was destined to be a hilarious disaster that went south quickly. [46]

It worked to get the fans in and over 25,000 fans showed up. Most didn't care about the game though, they just wanted to grab six beers for 60 cents then wobble back for seconds. Before long, everyone was totally sloshed.

In the second inning, things got really wild. A plus-sized lady flashed the crowd, then tried to plant one on the ump! Pandemonium! Fans started passing blunts and lighting firecrackers, turning the ballpark into a war zone. When the Rangers hit a dinger, a buck-naked dude slid into second. No one could catch this streaking bandit!

By now, the beer lines were longer than the Great Wall of China. The already trashed fans got straight up belligerent. That's when management, according to most opinions, threw gasoline on the fire by deciding to send the fans to the beer trucks outside!

The thirsty horde stampeded those trucks like wildebeests. Only two teenage girls were "guarding" them. Needless to say, they left faster than Roadrunner. With no supervision, fans treated the trucks like a personal kegger. Some even drank straight from the hoses!

Things were really getting out of hand. Two drunks pulled their pants down and started mooning the crowd, who thought it was hilarious. It was only the fifth inning! Half the game left and total anarchy had broken out.

When one of the Rangers got beaned, the crowd loved it and started chanting "Hit him harder!" Their manager Billy Martin -- with a well-known temper, came out arguing and cups started raining down. Then a barrage of firecrackers even cleared out the bullpen!

By the 9th inning, the stands were hurling anything they could find -- food, batteries, trash cans, seats! There were piles of abandoned clothes where streakers had been.

The Indians had only hired 50 people for security. Most of the staff bailed by the 8th. Finally, when Billy Martin grabbed a bat and rallied his team to fight the fans, it was clear -- this was the wildest, drunkest, craziest promotion in baseball history!

## So why is pickleball so popular and addictive?

There are a few reasons people seem to really enjoy it. Some say it's really easy to learn how to play. You don't need much training at all to get started. The court is also smaller than a tennis court, so it's more accessible. Pretty much anyone can play, including folks in wheelchairs.

Another reason is that it's a great workout. One study found that players had an average heart rate of 109 beats per minute and burned over 350 calories an hour. [47] That puts it on par with exercises like hiking, yoga, and water aerobics. And get this - after playing for an hour every other day for six weeks, players saw improvements in their cholesterol, blood pressure, and oxygen levels.

You can play indoors or outdoors too. You can play singles for a more intense workout, or doubles for fun with friends. It's also been said to be good for hand-eye coordination and neuromuscular skills.

If you've played tennis, ping pong, squash, or racquetball before, the techniques come pretty easily. As you play more, you start to get better at placing shots deep, dinking, smashing - you know, the fun stuff.

But really, for a lot of folks it just comes down to this - it's super fun to play!

**The Cursed Lions: When Fate Turned Against Detroit.** In the 1950s, the Detroit Lions were a force to be reckoned with. Under the leadership of quarterback Bobby Layne, they dominated their division, winning crowns in 1952, 1953, and 1954.

The 1953 title game would go down in sports lore. With less than five minutes left and the Browns ahead 16-10, Layne took command. As cool as could be, he orchestrated an 80-yard drive that culminated in a touchdown. Doak Walker's extra point kick gave the Lions an epic 17-16 comeback victory.

After a few years of success, turmoil struck. In 1957, Layne's coach left for Pittsburgh. The Lions still won it all that year with Layne at the helm. But the following year, in a shocking twist, Detroit traded their star quarterback to the Steelers as well.

Furious over the move, Layne made an ominous declaration. ***"The Lions will not win for 50 years,"*** he sneered to the press. And so, the "Curse of Bobby Layne" was born. From that moment on, an eerie shadow seemed to fall over the once mighty Lions. Over five decades, they failed to capture even one championship or experience lasting success. Layne's prophecy haunted Detroit to become one of the saddest sagas in pro football history.

**The Contest is What's the Best!** While others spend their days lost in the pursuit of trophies and titles, some seek deeper truths beneath the surface. For one man, the simple act of casting his line served not only to ensnare fish on the hook but also to snare greater insights from within. Beyond the shimmering scales and darting fins lay revelations that could only be found through patient contemplation amid the flowing waters.

Dreams know no boundaries if one is willing to reach beyond what is seen as possible.

For a champion, every challenge was an opportunity to soar to new heights. Records were meant to be shattered, limits were meant to be pushed, and goals once thought unattainable would be achieved through relentless effort and unbridled ambition. As long as the champion continues to envision greater accomplishments, the trajectory will only point upward and onward into the unknown.

While victory brings its rewards, loss is often the bitterest of pills. But even in defeat, there is dignity so long as one maintains composure and grace. Losing while keeping your fire burning inside is far preferable to surrendering your heart. Passion and pride can endure where scores alone do not.

The game had ended, yet debates would echo long into the night. For some, triumphing was hollow without validation, and finding fault in a loss was easier than owning up to your shortcomings.

But for true competitors, the contest itself is what brings the most joy -- the ups and downs, the ebbs and flows. It is the struggle that brings out our greatest qualities, and the lessons learned that last far beyond final tallies on the board.

# Answers to Quiz Questions

**1. A**. 1896. The Olympics are considered the biggest sports competition in the world. Over 200 different countries send teams to compete. It's usually considered the world championship for most sports that year.

The whole idea for the Olympics is, of course, based on ancient games they used to have in Greece. Pierre de Coubertin was inspired by them and started the International Olympic Committee in 1894. Then they held the first modern Olympics in Athens in 1896. It's a banner event in modern day worldwide.

The first Modern Olympics in 1896, Panathenaic Stadium, Athens.

**2. C**. A headless goat carcass. Sometimes they use a calf carcass. Besides playing buzkashi on horses, they also play it riding yaks especially those among the Tajiks of Xinjiang.

They usually play it on Fridays and matches draw thousands to watch. The object of the game is to seize control of the carcass and fight off rivals fairly or usually anyway they. In the early days matches would go on for days, but in the modern era there is usually a time limit.

Buzkashi

**3. C**. Lennox Lewis. Mike had a quick match against Louis Savarese, who's a mixed martial artist and boxer. Mike landed a big left hand in the first round that put Louis down right away. Louis did manage to get back up, but Mike just kept attacking him relentlessly. The referee John tried to step in after only 26 seconds, but Mike was still going and even took the ref down briefly.

Eventually Mike's corner got in the ring, and calmed Mike down. They called it a TKO win for Mike after just 38 seconds, which made it the second fastest fight of his career behind only his 30-second win over Marvis Frazier back in 1986.

After the fight Mike did an interview with Jim Gray from Showtime. He used the opportunity to call out Lennox Lewis, saying some wild, crazy stuff like "I want your heart, I want to eat your children. . ." Pretty intense stuff from Mike even after such a short fight! [48]

Mike Tyson

**4. F**. Running. All of the sports mentioned are very old sports that have been around for a long time. Evidence of the sports of running and wrestling were found dating back to 15,300 years ago and are probably the oldest sports in history. [49]

**5. D**. A man from the Czech Republic set that amazing record. His name is Josef Šálek, but his friends call him Joska. On May 20th of this year, Joska attempted the longest abdominal plank ever. And you know what? He actually did it! Can you believe he was able to hold a perfect plank position for over 9 hours straight? That's just nuts.

The Guinness Book of World Records has officially confirmed it - Joska held the plank for a total of 9 hours, 38 minutes, and 47 seconds. It's hard to imagine since your core muscles have to be absolutely shredded to withstand that kind of strain for so long. Most people can barely hold a plank for a couple minutes before collapsing. But Joska pushed through the pain and exhaustion for nearly 10 hours! His dedication and willpower are truly inspiring.

All that grueling training paid off big time. He must have been so relieved and proud when he finally dropped to the floor at the end. Joska enjoys the fame and recognition that comes with being in the Guinness Book. He definitely earned it after pulverizing his body for almost an entire day just to hold a plank. What an amazing feat of human strength and endurance!

**6. C**. Weightlifting. A "press out" will make the attempted lift not done. A press out happens when the weightlifter bends his or her arms while holding the bar overhead, then tries to make to make them straight. A press out is a no lift decision made by the judges in their discretion.

**7. D**. Monaco. Monaco had some incredible life expectancies according to that data from 2023! Both men and women there could expect to live to be quite old, into their 80s, with men reaching 84 years on average and women even higher at 89 years. Very amazing in our view if you think about it.

The East Asian countries of South Korea, Hong Kong, Macao, and Japan were right behind Monaco too in terms of life expectancy. Men in those places were living to around 81 years old on average, with women reaching 87 years.

It's also interesting to learn that football, or soccer as we call it here, is a big sport in the tiny country of Monaco. Of course, motor racing is huge there what with the famous Monaco Grand Prix. Yachting and tennis are highly popular as well.

And it makes sense - football is such a popular worldwide sport that of course the people of Monaco would enjoy it. The Monegasque Football Federation governs the game there. I wouldn't have expected such a small place to have its own football governing body, but it's great they have an organization dedicated to the sport.

# Index

## We hope you enjoyed the book!

Thank you for reading! If you liked the book, we would sincerely appreciate your taking a few moments to leave a brief review.

Thank you again very much!

Bruce Miller and Team Golfwell

*Thank You*

# About the author.

**Bruce Miller**. Lawyer, businessman, world traveler, private pilot, and award-winning author of over 50 books, a few being bestsellers, spends his days writing, studying, and constantly learning of the astounding, unexpected, and amazing events happening in the world today while exploring the brighter side of life.

Author of the Psychic Mystery/Thriller "Beware the Ides of March: A Novel Based on Psychic Readings" and awarded a 2023 NYC Big Book Distinguished Favorite.

He's a member of the Australian Golf Media Association, The New Zealand Society of Authors, and the Independent Book Publishers Association.

**Team Golfwell** are bestselling authors and founders of the very popular 370,000+ member Facebook Group "Golf Jokes and Stories."

Their books have sold thousands of copies including several #1 bestsellers in Golf Coaching, Sports humor, and other categories.

# We Want to Hear from You!

*"There usually is a way to do things better and there is opportunity when you find it." - Thomas Edison*

We love to hear your thoughts and suggestions on anything and please feel free to contact me at bruce@teamgolfwell.com

**Other Books by Bruce Miller**

Beware the Ides of March: A Novel Based on Psychic Readings (Awarded Distinguished Favorite by the NYC Big Book Award 2023).

Guy Wilson Creating Golf Excellence: The Genesis of Lydia Ko & More Stars

For a Great Fisherman Who Has Everything: A Funny Book for Fishermen

For the Golfer Who Has Everything: A Funny Golf Book

For a Tennis Player Who Has Everything: A Funny Tennis Book

The Funniest Quotations to Brighten Every Day: Brilliant, Inspiring, and Hilarious Thoughts from Great Minds

For Bright Legal Minds Who Have It All

And many more…

## References


[1] Frank Hayes (jockey), Wikipedia, https://en.wikipedia.org/wiki/Frank_Hayes_(jockey)
[2] Fighter lost, YouTube, https://www.youtube.com/watch?v=-lXOtEjRtEw
[3] Denise Mueller-Korenek is the Fastest Person on a Bike EVER, Bicycling, YouTube, https://youtube.com/watch?v=A6y_G_DJAzM
[4] MLB, McClendon ejected, takes first base https://www.youtube.com/watch?v=rhnoCkp2QUo
[5] Wellington Surfer Rode Out Giant Tsunami Waves, Stuff NZ, https://www.stuff.co.nz/world/south-pacific/2923467/Wellington-surfer-rode-out-giant-tsunami-waves
[6] HMY.com, https://www.hmy.com/biggest-fish-ever-caught/#:~:text=According%20to%20IGFA%20records%2C%20the,against%20this%20one%2Dton%20shark.
[7] Dragon Boat Tug of War, YouTube, https://www.youtube.com/watch?v=wmBJXHC6QEU
[8] 1News,YouTube, https://www.youtube.com/watch?v=fcQvAI07g7Y
[9] Independent, YouTube, https://www.independent.co.uk/sport/us-sport/referee-hits-player-in-ice-hockey-game-gets-mauled-by-teammates-a6757321.html
[10] Fastest speed for a racehorse, Guinness Book of World Records, https://www.guinnessworldrecords.com/world-records/fastest-speed-for-a-race-horse
[11] The fastest Race Horse: Winning Brew set a Guinness speed record - 43.97 mph, YouTube, https://www.youtube.com/watch?v=2G9PsYFSEk4
[12] KJRH TV, YouTube, https://www.youtube.com/watch?v=ESg5YDemMz4

[13] Jim's 1993 ESPY Speech, The V Foundation, YouTube, https://www.youtube.com/watch?v=HuoVM9nm42E
[14] Vanderbilt Tennis Club, https://vanderbilttennisclub.com/
[15] Micro Fishing for Tiny Fish With Tiny Telescoping Tanago Rod & Super Tiny Hooks, Fowlers Makery, YouTube, https://www.youtube.com/watch?v=CidZ-Hcbxsw
[16] Bob Feller, Wikipedia, https://en.wikipedia.org/wiki/Bob_Feller#:~:text=Feller%20once%20mentioned%20that%20he,in%201946%20at%20Griffith%20Stadium.
[17] Unraveling Steve Dalkowski's 110 MPH Fastball: The Making of the Fastest Baseball Pitcher, Bill Dembski, Everhttps://billdembski.com/book/unraveling-steve-dalkowskis-110-mph-fastball/
[18] Muhammad Ali, Amazing Speed, YouTube, C, https://www.youtube.com/watch?v=jkhpZoPOfZI
[19] Fastest recorded tennis serves, https://en.wikipedia.org/wiki/Fastest_recorded_tennis_serves
[20] The Guardian, https://www.theguardian.com/sport/2014/jul/30/sabine-lisicki-record-fastest-serve-women-tennis-stanford
[21] Ibid.
[22] Supra. SPCA
[23] The butt-fumble -- NFL on Thanksgiving, YouTube, https://www.youtube.com/watch?v=82RIfy-gRa4
[24] TRT World, What is Bossaball: the Best Sport You Never Heard of, YouTube, https://www.youtube.com/watch?v=4bF86FsaweY
[25] Jim Abbot, Wikipedia, https://en.wikipedia.org/wiki/Jim_Abbott
[26] Cotswold Olympics, Wikipedia, https://en.wikipedia.org/wiki/Cotswold_Olimpick_Games
[27] On Demand News, Gloucester hosts World Shin Kicking Championship, YouTube, https://www.youtube.com/watch?v=jN21wCbxjWk

[28] Unicycle Hockey, Wikipedia, https://en.wikipedia.org/wiki/Unicycle_hockey
[29] Ibid.
[30] Canadian woman wins UK's Cheese-Rolling race, unfazed by knockout: "Feels so good", Global News YouTube, https://www.youtube.com/watch?v=DmCaNFOfAew
[31] Bizarre 25, 25 examples of extreme ironing, YouTube, https://www.youtube.com/watch?v=j1y4rsEVzYo
[32] Lomu 1995 v. England, YouTube, https://www.youtube.com/watch?v=yhmQlxCDFSc&t=30s
[33] "He was IMPOSSIBLE to stop! | Jonah Lomu", World Rugby, YouTube, https://www.youtube.com/watch?v=nKoTGdIhO-U
[34]Baron Davis shot, YouTube, https://www.youtube.com/watch?v=7k1LCemWIdo, and https://www.youtube.com/watch?app=desktop&v=zWUEnbPsVfo
[35] Longest Basketball Shot Ever Thrown…, Guinness World Records, https://www.guinnessworldrecords.com/news/2022/8/longest-basketball-shot-ever-thrown-from-staggering-113-ft-716066
[36] Longest Home Run Hit, Guinness World Records, .https://www.guinnessworldrecords.de/world-records/64713-longest-home-run-hit
[37] "How much live action occurs in each sport? - Ball in Play studies summarized, Nationals Arm Race, https://www.nationalsarmrace.com/?p=475
[38] Leon de Lunden, Wikipedia, https://en.wikipedia.org/wiki/L%C3%A9on_de_Lunden
[39] The Stanley Cup, Wikipedia, https://en.wikipedia.org/wiki/Stanley_Cup
[40] Novak Djokovic, YouTube, https://www.youtube.com/watch?v=sUtQadqgxZo
[41] Dog makes incredible goal line save, FA 92, YouTube, https://www.youtube.com/watch?v=oaUH-nAg6UU

---

[42] King James I Assassination, Wikipedia, https://en.wikipedia.org/wiki/James_I_of_Scotland#Assassination

[43] Herald Zimbabwe, https://www.herald.co.zw/all-set-for-tiger-tournament/

[44] Ibid.

[45] Catching fish with a snake. https://www.youtube.com/watch?v=XDS2WWg9eZ4&feature=youtu.be

[46] Ten Cent Beer Night, Wikipedia, https://en.wikipedia.org/wiki/Ten_Cent_Beer_Night

[47] IJREP.org, “The Acute and Chronic Physiological Responses to Pickleball in Middle-Aged and Older Adults”, https://ijrep.org/the-acute-and-chronic-physiological-responses-to-pickleball-in-middle-aged-and-older-adults/

[48] Mike Tyson vs. Lou Savarese, Wikipedia, https://en.wikipedia.org/wiki/Mike_Tyson_vs._Lou_Savarese

[49] History of Sport, Wikipedia, https://en.wikipedia.org/wiki/History_of_sport

Printed in Great Britain
by Amazon

2e7d017a-de4e-4e7e-b632-2a9f24a71f59R01